ARM 54 Course Guide

Risk Assessment
3rd Edition

The Institutes
720 Providence Road, Suite 100
Malvern, Pennsylvania 19355-3433

3rd Edition • 5th Printing • July 2010

ISBN 978-0-89463-370-6

Contents

Study Materials Available for ARM 54

Etti G. Baranoff, Scott E. Harrington, and Gregory R. Niehaus, *Risk Assessment*, 1st ed., 2005, AICPCU/IIA.

ARM 54 *Course Guide,* 3rd ed., 2008, AICPCU/IIA (includes access code for SMART Online Practice Exams).

ARM 54 SMART Study Aids—Review Notes and Flash Cards, 3rd ed.

Student Resources

Catalog A complete listing of our offerings can be found in *Succeed,* the Institutes' professional development catalog, including information about:

- Current programs and courses
- Current textbooks, course guides, SMART Study Aids, and online offerings
- Program completion requirements
- Exam registration

To obtain a copy of the catalog, visit our Web site at www.TheInstitutes.org or contact Customer Service at (800) 644-2101.

How to Prepare for Institute Exams This free handbook is designed to help you by:

- Giving you ideas on how to use textbooks and course guides as effective learning tools
- Providing steps for answering exam questions effectively
- Recommending exam-day strategies

The handbook is printable from the Student Services Center on the Institutes' Web site at www.TheInstitutes.org, or available by calling Customer Service at (800) 644-2101.

Educational Counseling Services To ensure that you take courses matching both your needs and your skills, you can obtain free counseling from the Institutes by:

- E-mailing your questions to advising@TheInstitutes.org
- Calling an Institutes' counselor directly at (610) 644-2100, ext. 7601
- Obtaining and completing a self-inventory form, available on our Web site at www.TheInstitutes.org or by contacting Customer Service at (800) 644-2101

Exam Registration Information As you proceed with your studies, be sure to arrange for your exam.

- Visit our Web site at www.TheInstitutes.org forms to access and print the Registration Booklet, which contains information and forms needed to register for your exam.
- Plan to register with the Institutes well in advance of your exam.

How to Contact the Institutes For more information on any of these publications and services:

- Visit our Web site at www.TheInstitutes.org
- Call us at (800) 644-2101 or (610) 644-2100 outside the U.S.
- E-mail us at customerservice@TheInstitutes.org
- Fax us at (610) 640-9576
- Write to us at The Institutes, Customer Service, 720 Providence Road, Suite 100, Malvern, PA 19355-3433

Using This Course Guide

This course guide will help you learn the course content and prepare for the exam.

Each assignment in this course guide typically includes the following components:

Educational Objectives These are the most important study tools in the course guide. Because all of the questions on the exam are based on the Educational Objectives, the best way to study for the exam is to focus on these objectives.

Each Educational Objective typically begins with one of the following action words, which indicate the level of understanding required for the exam:

Analyze—Determine the nature and the relationship of the parts.

Apply—Put to use for a practical purpose.

Associate—Bring together into relationship.

Calculate—Determine numeric values by mathematical process.

Classify—Arrange or organize according to class or category.

Compare—Show similarities and differences.

Contrast—Show only differences.

Define—Give a clear, concise meaning.

Describe—Represent or give an account.

Determine—Settle or decide.

Evaluate—Determine the value or merit.

Explain—Relate the importance or application.

Identify or list—Name or make a list.

Illustrate—Give an example.

Justify—Show to be right or reasonable.

Paraphrase—Restate in your own words.

Recommend—Suggest or endorse something to be used

Summarize—Concisely state the main points.

Required Reading The items listed in this section indicate the study materials that correspond to the assignment.

Outline The outline lists the topics in the assignment. Read the outline before the required reading to become familiar with the assignment content and the relationships of topics.

Key Words and Phrases These words and phrases are fundamental to understanding the assignment and have a common meaning for those working in insurance. After completing the required reading, test your understanding of the assignment's Key Words and Phrases by writing their definitions.

Review Questions The review questions test your understanding of what you have read. Review the Educational Objectives and required reading, then answer the questions to the best of your ability. When you are finished, check the answers at the end of the assignment to evaluate your comprehension.

Application Questions These questions continue to test your knowledge of the required reading by applying what you've studied to "hypothetical" real-life situations. Again, check the suggested answers at the end of the assignment to review your progress.

Sample Exam Your course guide includes a sample exam (located at the back) or a code for accessing SMART Online Practice Exams (which appears on the inside back cover). Use the option available for the course you're taking to become familiar with the test format.

For courses that offer SMART Online Practice Exams, you can either download and print a sample credentialing exam or take full practice exams using questions like those that will appear on your credentialing exam. SMART Online Practice Exams are as close as you can get to experiencing an actual exam before taking one.

More Study Aids

The Institutes also produce supplemental study tools, called SMART Study Aids, for many of our courses. When SMART Study Aids are available for a course, they are listed on both page iii of this course guide and on the first page of each assignment. SMART Study Aids include Review Notes and Flash Cards and are excellent tools to help you learn and retain the information in each assignment.

ARM Advisory Committee

Patricia M. Arnold, CPCU, ALCM
University of Texas at Austin

Bryan W. Barger, CPCU, ARM, ALCM
Marsh USA, Inc.

Karen L. Butcher, ARM
Aon Risk Services, Inc. of Ohio

Dr. Richard B. Corbett, CLU, CPCU, ARM
Florida State University

Donald E. Dresback, CPCU, ARM, AAI
The Beacon Group, Inc.

Mary M. Eisenhart, CPCU, ARM, ARe
Agency Management—Resource Group

Elise M. Farnham, CPCU, ARM, AIM
Illumine Consulting

Edward S. Katersky, CPCU, ARM, CSP
BJ's Wholesale Club, Inc.

Melissa Olsen Leuck, ARM
TAP Pharmaceutical Products Inc.

Bill Mason, CPCU, ARM-P
Public Risk Management Association

Ludmilla Pieczatkowska, CPCU
William Gallagher Associates Insurance Brokers, Inc.

James Swanson, FIIC, RIMS Fellow
Government of Manitoba, Canada

Tom Worischeck, CSP, ARM
Kimmins Contrating Corp.

Understanding Risk Management and Establishing a Risk Management Program

Educational Objectives

After learning the content of this assignment, you should be able to:

1. Describe risk management and its broad scope.

2. Identify the costs and benefits of risk management for a particular organization and for the entire economy.

3. Describe the pre-loss and post-loss goals of a risk management program and the possible trade-offs among these goals.

4. Describe the risk management department structure, including:

   - Departments with which the risk management professional should cooperate and the types of information these departments provide

   - Communication of information into and out of the risk management department and organization

   - Information management and risk management information systems used to improve decision making

5. Describe the likely responsibilities and reporting relationships of a risk management professional.

6. Describe the purpose and content of a written risk management policy statement.

7. Explain how to monitor, and when appropriate to take corrective action to improve, the performance of an organization's risk management program through results standards and activity standards.

8. Define or describe each of the Key Words and Phrases for this assignment.

Study Materials

Required Reading:
▶ Risk Assessment
  • Chapter 1

Study Aids:
▶ SMART Online Practice Exams
▶ SMART Study Aids
  • Review Notes and Flash Cards—Assignment 1

Outline

▶ **Risk Management**
  A. Risk and Risk Management Defined
  B. Risk Management Scope
▶ **Risk Management Costs and Benefits**
  A. For a Particular Organization
    1. Reduced Cost of Risk
    2. Reduced Deterrence Effects
  B. For the Entire Economy
    1. Reduced Waste of Resources
    2. Improved Allocation of Productive Resources
▶ **Risk Management Program Goals**
  A. Pre-Loss Goals
    1. Economy of Operations
    2. Tolerable Uncertainty
    3. Legality
    4. Social Responsibility
  B. Post-Loss Goals
    1. Survival
    2. Continuity of Operations
    3. Profitability
    4. Earnings Stability
    5. Social Responsibility
    6. Growth
  C. Trade-Offs Among Goals

▶ **Risk Management Department Structure**
  A. Internal Structure
  B. Cooperation With Other Departments
  C. Communication
  D. Information Management and Risk Management Information Systems
▶ **Responsibilities and Reporting Relationships**
  A. Responsibilities
    1. Risk Management Program
    2. Risk Assessment
    3. Risk Control
    4. Risk Financing
  B. Reporting Relationships
▶ **Risk Management Policy Statement**
  A. Purpose
  B. Content
▶ **Risk Management Program Monitoring and Revising**
  A. Performance Standards
    1. Results Standards
    2. Activity Standards
  B. Actual Performance Versus Standards
  C. Corrective Action
▶ **Summary**

Don't spend time on material you have already mastered. The SMART Review Notes are organized by the Educational Objectives found in each course guide assignment to help you track your study.

▶▶

For each assignment, you should define or describe each of the Key Words and Phrases and answer each of the Review and Application Questions.

Educational Objective 1

Describe risk management and its broad scope.

Key Words and Phrases

Risk (p. 1.4)

Risk management (p. 1.5)

Business risk (p. 1.6)

Hazard risk (p. 1.6)

Loss exposure (p. 1.6)

Enterprise risk management (p. 1.6)

Review Questions

1-1.   Identify the possible meanings of risk apart from uncertainty about outcomes that can be either negative or positive. (p. 1.4)

1-2.   List the six steps in the risk management process. (pp. 1.4–1.5)

1-3.   Explain why risk management is an ongoing process. (p. 1.5)

1-4.   How does hazard risk differ from business risk? (p. 1.6)

1-5.   Explain how enterprise risk management differs from traditional risk management. (p. 1.6)

1-6.   Describe the four categories of risk used by some enterprise risk management models. (p. 1.7)

Application Question

1-7.   Using the enterprise risk management model described in the chapter, categorize the following risks:

a. Cost of materials increases.

b. Regulatory sanctions block the launch of a new product.

c. Securities and Exchange Commission investigate accounting practices.

d. Computer hackers steal confidential information.

e. Competitor hires key employees.

f. Customer files for bankruptcy.

g. Some consumers experience an allergic reaction.

h. Manufacturing facilities in Iraq are threatened by insurgents.

i. United States dollar falls against the euro, making the organization's debt more expensive to pay.

j. Union calls for a "sick-out."

k. Merger plans fall through.

l. Pollution.

m. Credit ratings reduced by a credit rating agency, resulting in
    increased cost of borrowing.

Educational Objective 2
Identify the costs and benefits of risk management for a particular organization and for the entire economy.

Key Word or Phrase
Cost of risk (p. 1.8)

Review Questions

2-1.   Identify the three broad categories of costs imposed by acciden-
       tal losses. (pp. 1.6–1.8)

2-2.   Identify what is included in an organization's cost of risk.
       (p. 1.8)

2-3.   Identify the benefits of risk management for the entire
       economy. (p. 1.10)

Application Question

2-4.   Using the data below, calculate the cost of risk. (p. 1.8)

Risk management department budget:	$ 1.2 million
Retained losses:	$10.5 million
Insurance premiums:	$20.0 million
Risk control techniques:	$ 5.0 million

Educational Objective 3

Describe the pre-loss and post-loss goals of a risk management program and the possible trade-offs among these goals.

Key Words and Phrases

Risk management program (p. 1.10)

Pre-loss goals (p. 1.11)

Post-loss goals (p. 1.11)

Review Questions

3-1.   Describe four pre-loss goals of a risk management program. (pp. 1.11–1.13)

3-2.   How might the economy of a risk management program be measured? (p. 1.11)

3-3.   Describe six post-loss goals of a risk management program. (pp. 1.13–1.17)

3-4.   Identify which goals of a risk management program generally require smaller commitments of an organization's resources. (p. 1.14)

3-5.   Identify the steps an organization should take to forestall an intolerable shutdown. (p. 1.15)

3-6.   Explain why continuity of operations is considered an essential goal for all public entities. (p. 1.16)

Application Questions

3-7.   The risk management professional of the Barnton Corporation is periodically consumed with anxiety regarding the effectiveness of the risk management program. Explain which of the program's pre-loss goals best addresses this risk management professional's concern. (pp. 1.11–1.13)

3-8.   Give an example of how each of the following risk management program goals conflict with the pre-loss goal of economy of operations: (pp. 1.17–1.18)

   a. Tolerable uncertainty

   b. Legality

   c. Social responsibility

Educational Objective 4

Describe the risk management department structure, including:

- Departments with which the risk management professional should cooperate and the types of information these departments provide

- Communication of information into and out of the risk management department and organization

- Information management and risk management information systems used to improve decision making

Review Questions

4-1.   Describe how a risk management department changes as an organization grows. (pp. 1.18–1.20)

4-2.   Identify departments that might provide information support to the risk management professional. (p. 1.21)

4-3.   Identify the types of information that might be communicated into and out of an organization's risk management department. (pp. 1.22–1.23)

4-4. Identify the ten ways that the quality of information can be described. (p. 1.24)

Application Question

4-5. Baby Crib Manufacturer is concerned that its risk management department is not getting all the information it needs to make sound decisions. Describe the information the risk management professional may expect from the following departments regarding risk management issues: (p. 1.21)

a. Legal

b. Marketing

c. Accounting

Educational Objective 5

Describe the likely responsibilities and reporting relationships of a risk management professional.

Review Questions

5-1.   Identify the four generic categories of risk management professionals' duties that are usually not delegated to others. (pp. 1.25–1.28)

5-2.   Identify the responsibilities of the risk management professional in an organization's risk management program. (pp. 1.25–1.26)

5-3.   Identify the responsibilities of the risk management professional in an organization's risk control efforts. (pp. 1.26–1.27)

5-4.   Identify the tasks the risk management professional must complete in an organization's risk financing program. (pp. 1.27–1.28)

Application Question

5-5. Through a leveraged buyout, Regional Department Store has purchased National Department Store. Explain how the risk management department of Regional Department Store may need to be restructured as a consequence of this organizational change. (pp. 1.18–1.20)

Educational Objective 6

Describe the purpose and content of a written risk management policy statement.

Key Word or Phrase

Risk management policy statement (p. 1.29)

Review Questions

6-1. What does a risk management policy statement communicate? (p. 1.29)

6-2. Describe the purpose of a written risk management policy statement. (p. 1.29)

6-3. Identify the typical content of a written risk management
      policy statement. (pp. 1.29–1.30)

Application Question

6-4. Using Exhibit 1-8 as a resource, create a risk management
      policy statement for a hospital providing trauma service to a
      rural community. (p. 1.31)

Educational Objective 7

**Explain how to monitor, and when appropriate to take corrective action to improve, the performance of an
organization's risk management program through results standards and activity standards.**

Key Words and Phrases

Results standards (p. 1.31)

Activity standards (p. 1.31)

Review Questions

7-1. Identify how results standards can be measured. (p. 1.31)

7-2. Describe three results that may occur when actual performance is compared with performance standards. (p. 1.31)

7-3. What conclusions might be drawn when performance substantially exceeds a standard? (p. 1.32)

Application Question

7-4. For each of the following, suggest a standard that a risk management professional might use to gauge performance:

a. Shipments to customers are damaged in transit.

b. Customers are injured when premises surfaces are wet.

c. Vehicles are damaged in backing incidents.

d. Employees are injured while cutting sheet metal.

Answers to Assignment 1 Questions

NOTE: These answers are provided to give students a basic understanding of acceptable types of responses. They often are not the only valid answers and are not intended to provide an exhaustive response to the questions.

Educational Objective 1

1-1.   The possible meanings of risk include the following:

- The subject matter of an insurance policy
- The insurance applicant (the insured)
- The possibility of a loss or injury
- A cause of loss (or peril)
- Variability associated with a future outcome

1-2.   The six steps in the risk management process are as follows:

(1) Identifying loss exposures

(2) Analyzing loss exposures

(3) Examining the feasibility of risk management techniques

(4) Selecting the appropriate risk management techniques

(5) Implementing the selected risk management techniques

(6) Monitoring results and revising the risk management program

1-3.   Risk management is an ongoing process because past choices of risk management techniques must be continually reevaluated in light of changes in the following:

- An organization's resources and activities and its resulting additional exposures to accidental loss
- Relative costs of alternative risk management techniques
- An organization's legal requirements
- An organization's goals
- The economic environment

1-4.   Hazard risk results in only two outcomes: loss or no loss. Business risk can result in either loss, no loss, or gain.

1-5.   Enterprise risk management differs from traditional risk management in the following ways:

- Enterprise risk management encompasses both hazard risk and business risk; traditional risk management focuses on hazard risk.
- Enterprise risk management seeks to enable an organization to fulfill its greatest productive potential; traditional risk management seeks to restore an organization to its former pre-loss condition.
- Enterprise risk management focuses on the value of the organization; traditional risk management focuses on the value of the accidental loss.
- Enterprise risk management focuses on an organization as a whole; traditional risk management focuses on specific loss exposures.

1-6. The four categories of risk used by some enterprise risk management models are as follows:

(1) Strategic risk—uncertainties associated with the organization's overall long-term goals and management

(2) Operational risk—uncertainties associated with the organization's operations

(3) Financial risk—uncertainties associated with the organization's financial activities

(4) Hazard risk—uncertainties associated with the organization's reduction in value resulting from the effects of accidental losses

1-7. Risk categorized using the enterprise risk management model shown in the chapter is as follows:

a. Cost of materials increases—operational risk.

b. Regulatory sanctions block the launch of a new product—strategic risk.

c. Securities and Exchange Commission investigate accounting practices—strategic risk.

d. Computer hackers steal confidential information—hazard risk.

e. Competitor hires key employees—strategic risk.

f. Customer files for bankruptcy—strategic risk.

g. Some consumers experience an allergic reaction—hazard risk.

h. Manufacturing facilities in Iraq are threatened by insurgents—strategic risk.

i. United States dollar falls against the euro making the organization's dollar more expensive to pay—financial risk.

j. Union calls for a "sick-out"—strategic risk.

k. Merger plans fall through—strategic risk.

l. Pollution—hazard risk.

m. Credit rating is reduced by a credit rating agency resulting in increased cost of borrowing—financial risk.

Educational Objective 2

2-1. The three broad categories of costs imposed by accidental losses are as follows:

(1) Reduction in property value, income, earning capacity, or quality of life because of damage, destruction, or injury

(2) Loss of net benefits that could have been gained from deterred activities

(3) Cost of resources devoted to managing accidental losses

2-2. An organization's cost of risk is the total of the following:

• Costs of accidental losses not reimbursed by insurance or other outside sources

• Insurance premiums or expenses incurred for noninsurance indemnity

• Costs of risk control techniques to prevent or reduce the size of accidental losses

• Cost of administering risk management activities

2-3. The benefits of risk management for the entire economy are as follows:

• Reduced waste of resources—risk management can prevent or minimize the waste of productive resources and the need to use productive resources to restore damage from accidental losses.

- Improved allocation of productive resources—risk management improves the willingness of management to undertake risky activities that might maximize profits, returns on investments, and wages.

2-4. The cost of risk is calculated as follows:

$1.2 million + $10.5 million + $20 million + $5 million = $36.7 million.

Educational Objective 3

3-1. Four pre-loss goals of risk management are as follows:

(1) Economy of operations—operate risk management economically and efficiently

(2) Tolerable uncertainty—keep managers' uncertainty about accidental losses at tolerable levels

(3) Legality—ensure that an organization's legal obligations are satisfied

(4) Social responsibility—act to promote ethical conduct and philanthropic commitments

3-2. The economy of a risk management program might be measured by comparing the organization's risk management costs with those of similar organizations (benchmarking), then relating these costs to revenue.

3-3. Six post-loss goals of risk management are as follows:

(1) Survival—no permanent halt to the organization's production, and key functional departments such as production, marketing, and finance continue unabated

(2) Continuity of operations—no significant interruption to the organization's operations

(3) Profitability—maintain a minimum level of profit or surplus through insurance and other means of transferring financial consequences

(4) Earnings stability—maintain a consistent earning level over time

(5) Social responsibility—continue activities to build community relationships and obligations

(6) Growth—protect expanding resources

3-4. The essential goals of a risk management program, such as survival and continuity of operations, generally require smaller resource commitments than do the desirable goals, such as social responsibility and growth.

3-5. An organization should take the following steps to forestall an intolerable shutdown:

- Identify activities whose interruptions cannot be tolerated
- Identify the types of accidents that could interrupt such activities
- Determine standby resources that must be immediately available to counter the effects of these accidents
- Ensure the availability of the standby resources

3-6. Continuity of operations is considered an essential goal for all public entities because any sustained interruption in services is likely to have serious consequences and interfere with the well-being of citizens and the community.

3-7. The risk management professional's concerns are best addressed by the pre-loss goal of tolerable uncertainty. The risk management program should anticipate and plan for accidental losses so that they will be effectively treated, thereby reducing uncertainty about accidental losses.

3-8.   The risk management program pre-loss goal of economy of operations conflicts with other risk management goals as follows:

    a.   Tolerable uncertainty might conflict with the goal of economy of operations because of the cost of risk management efforts.

    b.   Legality might conflict with the goal of economy of operations because some safety standards could require added expense to implement.

    c.   Social responsibility might conflict with the goal of economy of operations because obligations such as charitable contributions would raise added costs.

Educational Objective 4

4-1.   As an organization grows and the number of loss exposures increase, the internal structure of a risk management department may change. The rate at which staff is added depends on the organization's operations and management's attitude toward risk management. Small organizations often begin with a risk management director, a safety and loss prevention manager, and a claim manager. As more complex aspects of safety emerge and the number of claims increases, departmental expansion occurs—including adding risk financing personnel and specialized claim personnel.

4-2.   Departments that might provide information support to the risk management professional include the following:

- Accounting—provides historical cost information that helps determine current and replacement cost of physical assets and properties and provides information that helps determine continuing expenses and revenue reductions caused by a business interruption.

- Information Systems—tracks loss exposures and performs analytical evaluations that might reveal opportunities and threats to operations.

- Legal—offers advice on matters including liability claim management, product label wording, and procedures in the event of product failure.

- Human Resources—helps identify an organization's essential personnel.

- Production—provides information about essential processes, equipment, key suppliers, and customers.

- Marketing—provides information regarding product or service deficiencies.

4-3.   The types of information that might be communicated into and out of an organization's risk management department include the following:

- Loss exposure reports

- Bulletins on new or intensified loss exposures plus requests that all departments be especially alert to these new loss exposures

- Briefs from trade associations

- Reports from government agencies

- Information gathered from seminars on risk management techniques

- Data reported to trade associations or government agencies

- Facts or procedures that a risk management professional shares at professional meetings or through letters or articles submitted to risk management periodicals

- Direction as to how to report and analyze accidents and how to compile data about each department's risk management costs

- Government bulletins on setting standards for acceptable levels of safety, fire protection, or industrial hygiene
- Certifications indicating compliance with government standards
- Risk management annual report

4-4.   The ten ways that the quality of information can be described are as follows:

(1) Accessible—can the information be accessed easily and quickly?

(2) Comprehensive—is the information comprehensive?

(3) Accurate—is the information free from error?

(4) Appropriate—is the information relevant to the user's request or need?

(5) Timely—how current is the information?

(6) Clarity—how is the information presented?

(7) Flexible—how adaptable is the information?

(8) Verifiable—can the validity of the information be easily determined?

(9) Free from bias—has the information been free from any attempt to alter it in support of a preconceived conclusion?

(10) Quantifiable—to what extent is the information susceptible to mathematical manipulation?

4-5.   The risk management professional may expect the following information regarding risk management issues:

a.   Legal department—U.S. Consumer Product Safety Commission guidelines, case law, and past court cases involving baby cribs

b.   Marketing department—consumer reaction to crib safety features

c.   Accounting department—vendor of each model sold and where each model is being sold

Educational Objective 5

5-1.   The four generic categories of risk management professionals' duties that are usually not delegated to others are as follows:

(1) Risk management program

(2) Risk assessment

(3) Risk control

(4) Risk financing

5-2.   The responsibilities of the risk management professional in an organization's risk management program include the following:

- Guide senior management in establishing the organization's risk management program
- Plan, organize, lead, and control the resources and activities of the risk management department or function
- Assist senior management in establishing responsibility for, and channels of communication regarding, risk management matters
- Work with other managers to define the responsibilities and motivate those who implement the risk management program

- Apportion the costs of the risk management program equitably among the organization's departments and provide incentives for optimum risk management efforts

- Adapt the organization's risk management program and use risk control and financing techniques as loss exposures change and the cost of using those techniques changes

5-3.   The responsibilities of the risk management professional in an organization's risk control efforts include the following:

- Identifying the benefits and measuring and controlling the costs of alternative risk control techniques

- Coordinating the efforts to recognize hazards and implement appropriate risk control techniques

- Advising senior managers how to emphasize safety, to encourage and reward safe employee performance, and to correct shortcomings in risk control

- Informing middle managers how to fulfill their fundamental responsibilities for preventing accidents in their area of operation

- Helping middle managers implement risk control techniques

5-4.   The tasks the risk management professional must complete in an organization's risk financing program include the following:

- Work with financial and other senior executives to determine the extent to which the organization should retain losses and transfer potential losses

- Decide which retention and transfer techniques should be used to finance losses from specific loss exposures

- Negotiate to implement the chosen retention or transfer techniques

- Activate the appropriate retention or transfer techniques when a loss occurs

- Identify the benefits, as well as measure and control the costs, of alternative risk financing techniques to develop the most cost-effective risk financing program

5-5.   As a consequence of its acquisition of National Department Store, Regional Department Store's risk management department will likely be expanded. The roles of insurance manager, safety and loss prevention manager, claim manager, and security manager will be greater and will likely have personnel reporting to them. In addition, large risk management departments normally can justify having specialists, such as a safety supervisor or a fire protection supervisor.

Educational Objective 6

6-1.   A risk management policy statement communicates the goals of the risk management program and the roles that people throughout the organization have in achieving the organization's risk management goals.

6-2.   The purpose of a written risk management policy statement is to do the following:

- Establish the general goals of the organization's risk management function

- Define the responsibilities of risk management personnel

- Coordinate the treatment of loss exposures on a reasonably standardized basis among any organizational subdivisions

- Establish and improve existing communication channels and information management systems

- Provide for program continuity and facilitate transition during times of risk management personnel changes

6-3. A written risk management policy statement typically includes the following:

- General description of risk management and its importance to the organization
- Risk management department's internal structure
- Senior management's risk management goals
- Decision rules for selecting risk management techniques

6-4. Risk Management Policy Statement—Trauma Center

The Trauma Center recognizes its essential role in the rural community it serves. Consequently, the Trauma Center has established a risk management program that focuses on the post-loss objective of continuity of operations. While a more challenging and more expensive objective than merely survival in the face of potential hazard risk, Trauma Center's board believes it to be the right objective to pursue. Consequently, Trauma Center will do the following:

- Establish a risk management committee with representatives from all departments
- Implement the risk management process so that loss exposures may be assessed and monitored
- Support risk control and risk financing initiatives recommended by the risk management committee

The Trauma Center provides a range of services, all of which give rise to some level of risk. The Trauma Center is committed to regularly assessing and treating those risks to minimize their effect on service delivery. In this way, the Trauma Center will better achieve its goals and enhance the value of the services it provides. The underlying objectives of the Trauma Center's risk management program are to do the following:

- Embed risk management into the culture and operations
- Integrate risk management into service planning and performance management
- Manage risk in accordance with best practices
- Anticipate and respond to changing social, environmental, and legislative requirements
- Make sure that departments have clear accountability for both the ownership and cost of risk and the risk management techniques

These underlying objectives will be achieved by the following:

- Establishing clear roles, responsibilities, and reporting lines within the Trauma Center for risk management processes
- Incorporating risk management in the Trauma Center's decision-making, business planning, and performance management processes
- Monitoring the risk management program on a regular basis
- Reinforcing the importance of effective risk management through training
- Providing suitable insurance or other arrangements to manage the effect of unavoidable risk

Educational Objective 7

7-1. Results standards can be measured using dollars, percentages, ratios, or numbers of losses or claims. These standards focus on achievements regardless of the efforts required.

7-2. When actual performance is compared with performance standards, the following three results may occur:

- Meets established standards—usually the performance and standard are appropriate.
- Falls below established standards—corrective action is needed; performance is raised to the standard or a more realistic standard is set.
- Exceeds established standards—indicates exceptional performance or that the standards are too low or incomplete.

7-3. When performance substantially exceeds a standard, an organization might conclude that the standard was set too low, the standard was incomplete, or that the standard is appropriate and the performance is exceptional.

7-4. A risk management professional might use the following standards to gauge performance:
   a. Shipments to customers are damaged in transit—less than 5 percent of all shipments damaged in transit.
   b. Customers are injured when premises surfaces are wet—no customer injury claims when premises surfaces are wet.
   c. Vehicles are damaged in backing incidents—less than 5 percent of vehicle accidents resulting from backing up.
   d. Employees are injured while cutting sheet metal—no employee injuries while cutting sheet metal.

Direct Your Learning

Understanding the Risk Management Process

Educational Objectives

After learning the content of this assignment, you should be able to:

1. Identify the steps in the risk management process.

2. Describe the four types of loss exposures.

3. Describe the methods of identifying loss exposures.

4. Explain how to analyze loss exposures along the dimensions of loss frequency, loss severity, total dollar losses, timing, and data credibility.

5. Describe the following risk control techniques:

   - Avoidance
   - Loss prevention
   - Loss reduction
   - Separation
   - Duplication
   - Diversification

6. Describe the risk financing techniques of transfer and retention.

7. Explain how to select appropriate risk management techniques.

8. Describe the technical and managerial decisions that must be made to implement the selected risk management techniques.

9. Identify reasons why a risk management program may need to be revised.

10. Describe the concept of Enterprise Risk Management (ERM), including:

    - What it is
    - Why it works in theory
    - Why an organization should make it work
    - What frequently encountered impediments prevent or complicate its use in organizations

11. Define or describe each of the Key Words and Phrases for this assignment.

Study Materials

Required Reading:
- ▶ Risk Assessment
  - Chapter 2
- ▶ "Enterprise Risk Management," Course Guide Reading 2-1

Study Aids:
- ▶ SMART Online Practice Exams
- ▶ SMART Study Aids
  - Review Notes and Flash Cards—Assignment 2

Outline

▶ **Step One: Identifying Loss Exposures**

    A. Types of Loss Exposures

        1. Property Loss Exposures

        2. Liability Loss Exposures

        3. Personnel Loss Exposures

        4. Net Income Loss Exposures

    B. Methods of Identifying Loss Exposures

        1. Risk Assessment Questionnaires

        2. Loss Histories

        3. Financial Statements and Underlying Accounting Records

        4. Other Records and Documents

        5. Flowcharts and Organizational Charts

        6. Personal Inspections

        7. Expertise Within and Beyond the Organization

▶ **Step Two: Analyzing Loss Exposures**

    A. Loss Frequency

    B. Loss Severity

        1. Maximum Possible Loss (MPL)

        2. Probable Maximum Loss (PML)

        3. Loss Frequency and Loss Severity Interaction

        4. Total Dollar Losses

        5. Timing

        6. Data Credibility

▶ **Step Three: Examining the Feasibility of Risk Management Techniques**

    A. Risk Control Techniques

        1. Avoidance

        2. Loss Prevention

        3. Loss Reduction

        4. Separation, Duplication, and Diversification

    B. Risk Financing Techniques

        1. Transfer

        2. Retention

▶ **Step Four: Selecting the Appropriate Risk Management Techniques**

    A. Forecasts as the Basis for Selection

    B. Selection Criteria

        1. Financial Considerations

        2. Nonfinancial Considerations

▶ **Step Five: Implementing the Selected Risk Management Techniques**

    A. Technical Decisions

    B. Managerial Decisions

▶ **Step Six: Monitoring Results and Revising the Risk Management Program**

▶ **Summary**

▶ **Enterprise Risk Management (Course Guide Reading 2-1)**

Reduce the number of Key Words and Phrases that you must review. SMART Flash Cards contain the Key Words and Phrases and their definitions, allowing you to set aside those cards that you have mastered.

Reading 2-1

Enterprise Risk Management

Enterprise Risk Management (ERM) is a unique, holistic approach to managing risk. Learning what ERM is in comparison to traditional risk management, why ERM works in theory, why an organization should make ERM work, and what are the most frequently cited impediments to applying ERM is helpful to understanding and identifying ERM's potential organizational role.

I. What Is ERM?

Brokers, consultants, internal auditors, and risk management professionals are only a few of those who use varied descriptions of ERM. One of the most comprehensive descriptions has come from a vocal ERM supporter, the Federal Reserve Board. Former Federal Reserve Board Governor Susan Schmidt Bies has stated that:

> Enterprise-wide risk management looks within and across business lines and activities of the organization as a whole to consider how one area of the firm may affect the risks of other business lines and the enterprise as a whole. This approach is in marked contrast with the silo approach to risk management, which considers the risks of activities or business lines in isolation, without considering how those risks interrelate and affect other business lines. While individual business lines or activities should continue to enhance their own risk management practices, as organizations gain in complexity it is important to provide critical oversight that can come only from an enterprise-wide risk management approach.[1]

Whether the source of a risk is financial, hazard, operational, or strategic, risks managed separately are not the same when managed together. ERM is an approach that manages all risks together as a portfolio. It is based on a risk management professional taking a holistic perspective that examines all the risks facing an organization. In contrast, traditional risk management has

been described as an approach that encourages individual business unit managers to take a more limited view of risk and to focus only on those operational risks that directly affect their unit. Some risk management professionals have referred to this traditional approach as viewing risks in a silo. Although the ERM approach and the traditional risk management approach encourage viewing risks from different perspectives, they do not contradict each other. ERM is an enhancement and an evolution of traditional risk management. ERM, when it is effectively implemented, improves the ability of managers of individual units to coordinate their risk management efforts within an overall risk management plan for the entire organization.

However, ERM adds a further dimension. Traditional risk management has historically focused on pure risks whereby the only two possible outcomes are loss or no loss. ERM also manages speculative risks so that the possible outcomes also include gain. Consequently, part of what distinguishes ERM from traditional risk management is its goal of exploiting opportunities to increase gain and create value for the organization's stakeholders.

Over the last several years, many organizations have attempted to provide a framework that describes the key principles of ERM. In 2004, the Committee of Sponsoring Organizations of the Treadway Commission (COSO) published one attempt at providing such a framework. Despite COSO's efforts to include the opinions of experts from the finance, accounting, and auditing industries, this framework has been criticized by some risk management professionals as being too focused on the financial services industry. However, despite those concerns, COSO has provided a widely recognized framework on which to build an ERM program. COSO itself recognizes that its framework is meant to be just the beginning of the application of ERM and that more specific industry or organizational approaches will follow.[2] COSO's framework consists of the following eight interrelated components:

1. Internal environment—sets the tone and the basis for how risk is viewed and addressed within the organization and includes determining the organization's risk appetite.

2. Objective setting—ensures that management has a process in place to set objectives that support the organization's mission.

3. Event identification—identifies internal and external occurrences that affect whether an organization will meet its objective.

4. Risk assessment—analyzes risks in terms of frequency and severity as a basis for determining how they will be managed.

5. Risk response—management selects which risk management techniques to apply such as avoidance, loss prevention, loss reduction, retention, and transfer.

6. Control activities—establish procedures in the implementation of the risk responses.

7. Information and communication—identify and capture relevant information. It is then communicated in a timely manner and in a form that enables people to carry out their responsibilities.

8. Monitoring—monitors ERM in its entirety and makes corrections as necessary.[3]

A more specific framework or standard to delineate what ERM is to a specific organization is difficult to establish partly because each organization has its own unique profile of risks that causes the organization to use ERM for different purposes. For example, some organizations see ERM only as a program to help achieve compliance with the Sarbanes-Oxley Act (SOX) of 2002. Those organizations are likely to structure the framework of their ERM programs to mirror the law's requirements.

Other organizations may see ERM as a program to achieve or maintain a high financial rating from a rating agency, such as Standard and Poor's or A.M. Best. Those organizations will likely structure their ERM programs to satisfy the rating agency's ERM rating criteria.

Further, some governments have recognized the benefits that could be realized if an ERM standard was established and have developed a required, standard ERM structure for certain organizations within their jurisdictions. Australia and New Zealand created the first national standard in 1995. Canada created its own version in 1997. United Kingdom and Germany followed in 2000. Japan did the same in 2001. While SOX and other legal requirements from the New York Stock Exchange (NYSE) and the Securities Exchange Commission (SEC) may require certain actions from publicly traded corporations in the United States, currently, the U.S. has no legally mandated ERM standard.[4]

However, other ERM frameworks are available for organizations' use. A risk management professional should carefully study the range of alternatives before selecting any ERM framework.

II. Why Does ERM Work?

Three main theoretical concepts explain why ERM works: interdependency, correlation, and portfolio theory. The first concept, interdependency, has often been neglected in traditional risk management. Historically, risk was quantified and managed in separate silos. For example, hazard risks, such as those resulting in product recalls because of contaminated ingredients, and financial risks, such as those associated with an organization's stock price, are normally quantified and managed as unrelated risks. The silo management of these two categories of risks ignores any interdependencies and assumes that the two are statistically independent. Events are statistically independent if the probability of one event occurring does not affect the probability of a second event occurring. However, the traditional assumption of independence may not always be valid. When it isn't valid, the assumption may result in an inefficient treatment of an organization's portfolio of risks.

ERM does not make the assumption that those two risks, or any risks, of an organization are unrelated. The product recall in the above example could have a direct and substantially negative effect on an organization's stock price.

Risk interdependency can also occur between two or more risks because of the inflation effect. The inflation effect on risk occurs when the sum of individual risk effects is less than the total effect from the combination of all risks. This is best understood through an example. Assume an organization incurs the following three losses within the same fiscal period:

- An explosion destroys an organization's primary production plant;
- The Federal Reserve Board raises short-term interest rates; and
- A competitor files suit against the organization, claiming patent infringement.

Taking each of these events in isolation (without regard for all three occurrences), the organization would have a suitable risk management financial response. The organization could use property insurance for the hazard risk of the plant explosion. The financial risk of a rising interest rate could be hedged with derivatives. The organization could use intellectual property insurance for the costs incurred in the patent infringement suit.

The organization could be prepared to bear the risk financing expenses such as deductibles and other uninsured costs. However, the combined effect of the losses occurring within the same fiscal period could produce an unanticipated and more severe result. This could occur, for example, when the explosion at the primary production plant caused the inventory and then the sales to drop precipitously. The resulting weaker fiscal position would negatively affect the firm's ability to negotiate favorable terms on a loan, particularly when the interest rates went up. These two events would result in the interest-rate derivative being inadequate. Further, the explosion may have destroyed the engineering plans that were the organization's best defense in the patent infringement suit.

The individual risk financing responses may have been adequate had all three losses not occurred within the same fiscal period. With an ERM program in place, the organization would improve its ability to recognize and manage the potentially catastrophic interdependency of losses before their occurrence.

The second concept that explains why ERM works is correlation. Correlation is the proposition that all risks facing an organization are either associated to some degree with each other or they are not at all associated. Correlation is the degree to which two or more risks respond to the same stimulus in terms of severity. For example, a high degree of correlation exists between earthquakes and tsunamis. A small earthquake is associated with a small series of waves; a large earthquake is associated with a large tsunami. Risk management professionals have gained an appreciation of the effect that correlation has on an organization's ability to manage risk. Additionally, knowing whether some risks are not correlated is also important to risk management professionals. Uncorrelated risks check or counterbalance the effects of other risks' intrinsic volatility. This process is referred to as internal hedging. ERM works, in part, because of the appreciation of, and management of, risk correlations.

The third concept that makes ERM work is portfolio theory. In an ERM context, a portfolio is a combination of risks. The combination of risks creates a portfolio that has less volatility (risk) than the sum of the individual components' volatility (risk). The desired stability is possible if the portfolio's combination of risks is balanced or diversified. In a well-diversified portfolio, one loss is balanced (hedged) by a gain in another risk (opportunity). Consequently, risks can be combined and more effectively managed as part of a portfolio of risks.[5]

III. Why Should an Organization Make ERM Work?

Some organizations see ERM as a method to comply with SOX. These organizations are concerned that without an ERM program in place, senior management will be unable to provide the necessary SOX certifications. Few members on an organization's board of directors are likely to forget that SOX Section 404 makes them personally liable for their actions. The penalties are up to 20 percent of the director's net worth and possible jail time. Moreover, the threat of a failure to comply with SOX has reduced the number of qualified directors willing to serve on boards. Fortunately, a well-documented and executed ERM program serves as a keep-out-of-jail card. Therefore, compliance with SOX is a strong driver motivating boards to adopt an ERM framework.

Also, the New York Stock Exchange (NYSE) and the Securities Exchange Commission (SEC) have regulations that require organizations whose stock is publicly traded on exchanges to have their senior management certify their knowledge of their organization's current and future risks. They must further certify that specific programs are in place to address those risks. Compliance with these regulations is consequently a driver motivating publicly traded corporations to use ERM.

Some organizations see ERM as a program to achieve or maintain a high financial rating from a rating agency such as Standard and Poor's or A.M. Best. These rating agencies have created ERM criteria they use to grade an organization's efforts in its use of ERM to manage risks. Therefore, achieving optimal financial ratings is a driver to adopt ERM.

Additionally, there appears to be a high correlation between compliance with government and rating agency requirements and improved management accountability and financial transparency (disclosure). In the wake of recent corporate malfeasance, such as improper accounting and improper disclosure, ERM has become a priority for many of an organization's stakeholders.

ERM implementation is also credited for creating a competitive advantage. One advantage is enabling an organization to exploit opportunities not identified by competitors. A second competitive advantage is a more efficient risk management program. For example, ERM can lower an organization's cost of risk due in part to the following:

1. Application of the portfolio theory;
2. Better coordination and integration of risk management, which prevents gaps and duplication of effort. For example, by realigning an organization's insurance coverages into a multi-risk integrated plan, an organization can reduce or eliminate multiple placements; and
3. Enhanced ability to meet an organization's strategic objectives.

IV. What Are the Most Frequently Cited Impediments to Applying ERM?

It may be surprising to learn that, despite its advantages, ERM has not been fully embraced by many organizations outside of the financial services industry. Perhaps the single biggest impediment to implementing ERM is the inability to quantify ERM's economic benefits. Many experts claim the reason why financial service organizations have been relatively quick to implement ERM is because many of their most critical operational risks, such as the risk a debtor will not repay a loan, are easily quantifiable with readily available empirical data. In contrast, the risk philosophies of many organizations place a high importance on other risks, such as reputational, political, or economic, that do not have abundant empirical data available. Consequently, some corporate executives are understandably reluctant to make a deeper commitment to using ERM without a clear and quantifiable business case.[6]

Corporate culture and turf wars have also been frequently cited as reasons why ERM has been difficult to implement. ERM requires the combined knowledge and focus from the people in diverse functions across an organization.

Unfortunately, reluctance to share trade secrets, intradepartmental jargon, managers' actions to defend their areas of responsibility from perceived attack, and the lack of senior management's clearly articulated support for ERM are recognized as sources of these problems. Some of the sources are relatively easy to overcome with senior management's help.

A last impediment to adopting ERM, discussed here, is technological deficiency. For ERM to be successful, the relevant people have to get the right information. For many organizations, those relevant people are in management. Management has to get information on all of the risks facing the organization in a timely and concise manner. Information that is too late to act on has marginal value. Likewise, receiving too much information whereby critical facts are camouflaged by voluminous amounts of less-important data hinders effective decision making. Management needs to be able to take a quick "dashboard" look at the critical risks affecting an organization. To create this dashboard capability, the risk management professional often needs assistance from Information Technology (IT). Applied IT systems enable the risk management professional to collect hazard risk data and to integrate this information with financial, operational, and strategic risk data. The goal is to integrate all the information so that it can be analyzed and put into a format that management can act on. Integrating the information in an Enterprise Risk Management Information System (ERMIS) has proven to be a daunting task. Fortunately, improvements in this technology are rapidly occurring. Some vendors have introduced comprehensive ERMIS software systems.

The solutions to many impediments in adopting ERM may be just over the horizon. When the solutions are found, they will likely be different for each organization. This is in large part because each organization has its own unique risk profile and risk philosophy. That is one of the reasons why implementation of ERM by a specific organization is still more of an art than a science.

Reading Notes

1. Susan Schmidt Bies, statement at the Risk Management Association and Consumer Bankers Association Retail Risk Conference (Chicago, July 16, 2004).

2. Michael J. Moody, "ERM's Future is Brighter," *Rough Notes*, vol. 148, issue 2 (February 2005): pp. 42–43.

3. http://www.coso.org/Publications/ERM/ COSO_ERM_ExecutiveSummary.pdf (accessed April 8, 2007).

4. Stephan R. Leimberg et al., *The Tools & Techniques of Risk Management & Insurance* (Cincinnati: National Underwriter Co., 2002) p. 7.

5. "Trends: Enterprise Risk Management A Review of the Basics," International Risk Management Institute, Inc., (November 2000), http:// www.irmi-online.com (accessed June 6, 2007).

6. Michael J. Moody, "Unlocking ERM's Potential," *Rough Notes*, vol. 148, issue 12 (December 2005): pp. 26–27.

For each assignment, you should define or describe each of the Key Words and Phrases and answer each of the Review and Application Questions.

Educational Objective 1
Identify the steps in the risk management process.

Review Questions

1-1.   Describe what the risk management process does for an organization. (p. 2.3)

1-2.   List the six steps in the risk management process. (p. 2.3)

1-3.   Describe how a risk management professional identifies loss exposures that could interfere with an organization's goals. (p. 2.3)

Application Question

1-4. Furniture Manufacturer acquires Furniture Store, a small
retail chain. How should the risk management professionals at
Furniture Manufacturer assess the acquisition? (p. 2.3)

Educational Objective 2
Describe the four types of loss exposures.

Key Words and Phrases

Property loss exposure (p. 2.4)

Tangible property (p. 2.4)

Real property (p. 2.4)

Personal property (p. 2.4)

Intangible property (p. 2.4)

Liability loss exposure (p. 2.5)

Personnel loss exposure (p. 2.5)

Net income loss exposure (p. 2.6)

Review Questions

2-1.   List the elements of every loss exposure. (p. 2.3)

2-2.   List the four types of loss exposures. (p. 2.4)

2-3.   Identify the two ways in which a liability loss exposure can cause actual loss. (p. 2.6)

Application Question

2-4. Two of the property loss exposures facing the owner of a particular jewelry store are (1) the possibility that a fire will destroy the building and all its contents and (2) that a robber will steal all the money in the store's cash register. Briefly describe the differences between these two loss exposures in terms of each of the following elements of every loss exposure:

a. The financial values exposed to loss

b. The causes of loss (perils)

c. The potential financial consequences of the loss

Educational Objective 3

Describe the methods of identifying loss exposures.

Key Words and Phrases

Balance sheet (p. 2.8)

Income statement (p. 2.8)

Statement of cash flows (p. 2.8)

Flowchart (p. 2.10)

Organizational chart (p. 2.11)

Review Questions

3-1. List the methods of identifying loss exposures. (p. 2.6)

3-2. Identify a strength and a weakness of risk assessment
       questionnaires. (p. 2.7)

3-3. Describe how a risk management professional can use each of
       the following financial statements to identify an organization's
       loss exposures:

       a. Balance sheet (p. 2.8)

b. Income statement (p. 2.8)

c. Statement of cash flows (p. 2.8)

Application Question

3-4. Retail Department Store's risk management professionals develop a loss history. What conclusions might be reached from reviewing the following excerpt from the loss history concerning a snowstorm on January 2?

Date	Incident	Paid
01/02	Customer injured back in a slip-and-fall.	$ 500
01/02	Customer broke arm in a slip-and-fall.	1,000
01/02	Customer cut head when she fell in store foyer.	200
01/02	Employee injured clearing snow in parking lot.	2,000
01/02	Employee-operated snow plow damages customer cars.	45,000

Educational Objective 4

Explain how to analyze loss exposures along the dimensions of loss frequency, loss severity, total dollar losses, timing, and data credibility.

Key Words and Phrases

Loss frequency (p. 2.12)

Law of large numbers (p. 2.13)

Loss severity (p. 2.13)

Maximum possible loss (MPL) (p. 2.13)

Probable maximum loss (PML) (p. 2.13)

Prouty approach (p. 2.14)

Review Questions

4-1. Describe the five dimensions used in loss exposure analysis. (p. 2.12)

4-2. Explain the difference between maximum possible loss (MPL) and probable maximum loss (PML) and identify the usefulness of these estimates in analyzing property or liability loss exposures. (pp. 2.13–2.14)

4-3. Describe the Prouty approach and how it is used by a risk management professional in analyzing loss frequency and loss severity. (p. 2.14)

Application Question

4-4. Trucking Company's risk management professional uses a Prouty chart when determining how to treat loss exposures. Place each of the following loss exposures in the most appropriate place in the Prouty chart:

a. Trucks bump the loading dock when preparing to load and unload.

b. The truck terminal is within half a mile of the Mighty River.

c. Trucks collide with other vehicles.

Loss Severity		Loss Frequency			
		Almost Nil	Slight	Moderate	Definite
	Severe				
	Significant				
	Slight				

Educational Objective 5

Describe the following risk control techniques:

- Avoidance
- Loss prevention
- Loss reduction
- Separation
- Duplication
- Diversification

Key Words and Phrases

Risk control (p. 2.18)

Avoidance (p. 2.18)

Loss prevention (p. 2.19)

Loss reduction (p. 2.19)

Separation (p. 2.20)

Duplication (p. 2.20)

Diversification (p. 2.20)

Review Questions

5-1. Distinguish between the risk control techniques of proactive avoidance and abandonment. (p. 2.18)

5-2. Distinguish between the risk control techniques of loss prevention and loss reduction. (p. 2.19)

5-3. Distinguish among the risk control techniques of separation, duplication, and diversification. (p. 2.20)

Application Question

5-4. Give an example of how an organization might use the following risk management techniques to manage fire loss exposures to real property:

a. Avoidance

b. Loss prevention

c. Loss reduction

Educational Objective 6
Describe the risk financing techniques of transfer and retention.

Key Words and Phrases

Risk financing (p. 2.21)

Insurance (p. 2.21)

Noninsurance risk transfer (p. 2.22)

Hold-harmless agreement (p. 2.22)

Hedging (p. 2.22)

Futures contract (p. 2.22)

Retention (p. 2.22)

Pre-loss funding (p. 2.23)

Current-loss funding (p. 2.23)

Post-loss funding (p. 2.23)

Review Questions

6-1. Describe the following noninsurance risk transfer techniques and provide examples of each:

a. Hold-harmless agreement (p. 2.21)

b. Hedging (p. 2.22)

6-2. Describe the following general methods used to fund retained
       losses:

       a. Pre-loss funding (p. 2.23)

       b. Current-loss funding (p. 2.23)

       c. Post-loss funding (p. 2.23)

6-3. Explain the basic distinction between transfer and retention as
       a means of risk financing. (p. 2.21)

Application Question

6-4.   A building owner contracts with a window cleaner for the cleaner to wash the exterior windows of the building each month. The contract contains a clause under which the window cleaner agrees to reimburse the building owner for any claims the building owner may have to pay because of damage or injury that the window cleaner's activities may cause to property or persons in the parking lot surrounding the building. Explain whether this agreement is an effective means of risk transfer. (p. 2.22)

Educational Objective 7

Explain how to select appropriate risk management techniques.

Review Questions

7-1.   Identify two processes used to select appropriate risk management techniques to achieve organizational goals. (p. 2.25)

7-2.   Identify the three different forecasts that must be made so that an organization can evaluate its ability to fulfill its goals. (p. 2.25)

7-3.   Explain the cash flow implications of implementing risk
        financing techniques. (p. 2.26)

Application Question

7-4.   For each of the following situations, identify the risk control
        technique being applied: (pp. 2.18–2.20)

   a. Model Rocket Manufacturer operates three isolated
       structures where rocket engines (cardboard tubes and
       explosive power) are assembled.

   b. Building Contractor assembles a shield made of scaffolding
       and plywood over the sidewalk before beginning extensive
       structural restoration of an office building.

   c. Shopping Mall retrofits all of its stores and public areas with
       a sprinkler system.

d. Baby Products Manufacturer stops making baby carriages because product-related injuries are highly susceptible to litigation.

e. Computer Chip Manufacturer relies extensively on one particular machine for building computer chips. Consequently, Computer Chip Manufacturer purchases a second machine in case there are problems with the one they usually use.

Educational Objective 8

Describe the technical and managerial decisions that must be made to implement the selected risk management techniques.

Review Questions

8-1. Explain why a risk management professional must consider the technical and managerial decisions that will support the implementation of a risk management technique. (p. 2.27)

8-2.   What technical decisions might a risk management professional make in implementing a decision to insure a loss exposure? (p. 2.27)

8-3.   Explain why a risk management professional must work cooperatively with others in the organization to implement risk management techniques. (pp. 2.27–2.28)

Application Question

8-4.   Financial Intermediary has broadened its view of risk management to include enterprise risk management. As a consequence, the senior risk management professional has been promoted to Chief Risk Officer (CRO), and she has been given the authority to develop and implement an enterprise risk management strategy. Why would working cooperatively with other managers be important for the CRO?

Educational Objective 9

Identify reasons why a risk management program may need to be revised.

Review Questions

9-1. What may serve as a basis for monitoring the risk management program? (p. 2.28)

9-2. Identify the situations that may necessitate a revision in an organization's risk management program. (p. 2.28)

9-3. Describe the necessary process an organization must conduct if a revision is required. (p. 2.28)

Application Question

9-4. Department Store's risk management professionals are satisfied with the techniques included in the store's risk management program. Changes in the insurance market have resulted in significant price increases. How may this affect Department Store's risk management program? (p. 2.28)

Educational Objective 10

Describe the concept of Enterprise Risk Management (ERM), including:

- What it is
- Why it works in theory
- Why an organization should make it work
- What frequently encountered impediments prevent or complicate its use in organizations

Review Questions

10-1.   Identify three theoretical concepts that explain why Enterprise Risk Management (ERM) works. (Course Guide Reading 2-1, p. 2.4)

10-2.   Why is it important for a risk management professional to know when risks are not correlated? (Course Guide Reading 2-1, p. 2.5)

10-3.   Corporate culture and turf wars are frequently cited as impediments to implementing ERM; what are some of the sources of these problems? (Course Guide Reading 2-1, pp. 2.6–2.7)

Application Question

10-4. The CEO of Large Pharmaceutical Company, whose stock is publicly traded on the NYSE and is in a competitive struggle to maintain market share for several of its key drugs, is trying to create buy in among her management for the implementation of an ERM program in her company. She has decided to start first by describing the drivers motivating other organizations to adopt their own ERM program. What are some of the drivers, applicable to her company, that she might tell her management about? (Course Guide Reading 2-1, p. 2.6)

Answers to Assignment 2 Questions

NOTE: These answers are provided to give students a basic understanding of acceptable types of responses. They often are not the only valid answers and are not intended to provide an exhaustive response to the questions.

Educational Objective 1

1-1.   The risk management process provides a methodology for assessing and treating accidental loss exposures to enable an organization to meet its pre-loss and post-loss goals.

1-2.   The six steps in the risk management process are as follows:
   (1)   Identifying loss exposures
   (2)   Analyzing loss exposures
   (3)   Examining the feasibility of risk management techniques
   (4)   Selecting the appropriate risk management techniques
   (5)   Implementing the selected risk management techniques
   (6)   Monitoring results and revising the risk management program

1-3.   A risk management professional identifies loss exposures by logically classifying all possible loss exposures and employing methods to identify specific loss exposures that could interfere with the organization's goals.

1-4.   Furniture Manufacturer's risk management professionals should assess the new acquisition using the six steps in the risk management process. Even if a risk management program is already in place at Furniture Store, Furniture Manufacturer's risk management program should be reevaluated in light of the loss exposures acquired.

Educational Objective 2

2-1.   Every loss exposure contains the following elements:
   • Financial value exposed to loss
   • Cause of loss (peril)
   • Potential financial consequences of that loss

2-2.   The four types of loss exposures are:
   (1)   Property loss exposures
   (2)   Liability loss exposures
   (3)   Personnel loss exposures
   (4)   Net income loss exposures

2-3.   A liability loss exposure can cause actual loss to an organization in the following two ways:
   (1)   Whenever the organization is sued for having breached a legal duty, allegedly harming another, the organization's loss consists of any money paid to the claimant plus expenses incurred for investigating or defending the claim.
   (2)   If found to be in breach of contract, the organization becomes contractually obligated to pay damages for any loss that the other party has suffered.

2-4. The differences between the jewelry store's two loss exposures (fire and burglary) in terms of each element of a loss exposure include the following:

a. The values exposed to loss from fire include the value of the building, inventory, personal property, and improvements. The values exposed to loss from robbery include the value of the money held in the store's cash register.

b. The causes of loss (perils) are fire and robbery.

c. The potential financial consequences of a fire include reduction in the value of the property, income lost during reconstruction or repair of the building, and possible additional costs of satisfying current building codes. The potential financial consequences of a robbery include loss of the value of the cash and reduction of income.

Educational Objective 3

3-1. The methods of identifying loss exposures are as follows:

- Risk assessment questionnaires
- Loss histories
- Financial statements and underlying accounting records
- Other records and documents
- Flowcharts and organizational charts
- Personal inspections
- Expertise within and beyond the organization

3-2. A strength of risk assessment questionnaires is that they can be answered by persons with minimal risk management expertise. A weakness is that respondents likely just answer the questions and do not offer additional relevant information.

3-3. The risk management professional can use the following financial statements to identify an organization's loss exposures:

a. Balance sheet—lists the organization's assets, liabilities, and net worth as of a particular date. A risk management professional can use this financial statement to identify property values and to identify the organization's legal obligations.

b. Income statement—shows the profit or loss for a specific period. A risk management professional can use this statement to identify net income loss exposures.

c. Statement of cash flows—shows cash receipts and cash payments during a specified period. A risk management professional can use this statement to determine the amount of excess resources available to cover retained accidental losses.

3-4. From Retail Store's loss history, the risk management professional can determine that a snowstorm on January 2 was the underlying cause for several accidents. Because so many instances occurred, the loss history might indicate that the snowstorm was a significant event to which Retail Store could not respond fast enough or failed to respond adequately.

Educational Objective 4

4-1. The five dimensions used in loss exposure analysis are as follows:

(1) Loss frequency—the number of losses that occur within a specified period

(2) Loss severity—the amount, in dollars, of a loss for a specific occurrence

(3) Total dollar losses—total dollar amount of losses for all occurrences during a specified period

(4) Timing—when losses occur and when loss payments are made

(5) Data credibility—the confidence that can be placed on available data to indicate future losses

4-2. Maximum possible loss (MPL) is an estimate of the largest possible loss that might occur. Probable maximum loss (PML) is the value of the largest loss that is likely to occur. MPL is more useful for analyzing property loss exposures than liability loss exposures because it is difficult to predict liability loss exposures. PML is more useful when estimating potential loss severity.

4-3. The Prouty approach is a subjective risk exposure analysis method used to evaluate loss frequency and loss severity. A risk management professional classifies loss exposures using four categories of loss frequency (almost nil, slight, moderate, definite) and three categories of loss severity (slight, significant, severe). This method provides the risk management professional with a means of prioritizing loss exposures, leading to risk treatment suggestions.

4-4. The loss exposures should be placed in the Prouty chart as follows:

		Loss Frequency			
		Almost Nil	**Slight**	**Moderate**	**Definite**
Loss Severity	**Severe**	b.			
	Significant			c.	
	Slight			a.	

Educational Objective 5

5-1. Proactive avoidance occurs when an organization decides not to incur a loss exposure in the first place. Abandonment occurs when an organization decides to eliminate a loss exposure that already exists.

5-2. Loss prevention reduces the frequency (or the likelihood) of a particular loss. Loss reduction reduces the severity (or the magnitude) of a particular loss.

5-3. Separation disperses a particular activity or asset over several locations and regularly relies on that asset or activity as part of the organization's working resources. Duplication uses backups, spares, or copies of critical property, information, or capabilities and keeps them in reserve. Diversification spreads loss exposures over numerous projects, products, markets, or regions.

5-4. An organization can use the following risk management techniques to manage fire loss exposures to real property:

a. Avoidance—an organization can avoid fire damage to a building (real property) that it needs for its operations by leasing the building rather than owning it.

    b.   Loss prevention—an organization can reduce the frequency of a fire loss to a building by implementing loss prevention procedures such as controlling processes that produce heat (sanding, welding, cooking, and so forth) and isolating these heat sources from flammable materials (saw dust, paper, grease, and so forth).

    c.   Loss reduction—an organization can reduce the severity of a fire loss to a building by implementing loss reduction measures such as minimizing the quantity of finished goods kept in the production area.

Educational Objective 6

6-1.   Examples of noninsurance risk transfer techniques include the following:

    a.   Hold-harmless agreement—a transfer of all or part of the financial consequences of loss to another party through a contract in which one party (the indemnitor) agrees to assume the liability of a second party (the indemnitee), such as when work is subcontracted or when property is leased

    b.   Hedging—a financial transaction in which an asset is held to offset the risk associated with another asset, such as a gambler betting both outcomes of a baseball game

6-2.   a.   Pre-loss funding—money to fund retained losses is set aside in advance of losses.

    b.   Current-loss funding—money to fund retained losses is provided at the time of the loss or immediately after it occurs.

    c.   Post-loss funding—retained losses are paid after the losses occur and borrowing or another method of raising additional capital is used in the meantime.

6-3.   Risk transfer shifts the potential burden of paying losses to another entity (such as an insurer). Risk retention requires the organization generate funds from within the organization to pay for losses.

6-4.   A clause under which the window cleaner agrees to reimburse the building owner for any claims the building owner may have to pay transfers only the financial consequences of losses. The agreement with window cleaner is contractual risk transfer. The effectiveness of this agreement depends on the window cleaner's ability to pay for losses that occur.

Educational Objective 7

7-1.   Two processes used to select appropriate risk management techniques to achieve organizational goals are as follows:

    (1) Forecasting the effects that the available risk management techniques are likely to have on the organization's ability to fulfill its goals and the costs of those techniques

    (2) Defining and applying selection criteria that measure how well each alternative risk management technique contributes financially and nonfinancially to organizational goals

7-2.   The three different forecasts that must be made so that an organization can evaluate its ability to fulfill its goals are as follows:

    (1) A forecast of the frequency and severity of the future losses

    (2) A forecast of the effects that various risk control and risk financing techniques are likely to have on the frequency, severity, and probability of future losses

    (3) A forecast of the costs of these techniques

7-3. Risk financing techniques often require cash outflows. However, these techniques also reduce other cash outflows caused by losses and may even generate cash inflows from others, such as insurers and indemnitors.

7-4. Appropriate risk control techniques might include the following:

    a.   Model Rocket Manufacturer—separation

    b.   Building Contractor—loss prevention

    c.   Shopping Mall—loss reduction

    d.   Baby Products Manufacturer—avoidance

    e.   Computer Chip Manufacturer—duplication

Educational Objective 8

8-1. A risk management professional must consider technical and managerial decisions so that the selected risk management technique can be successfully implemented. Technical decisions include how to implement a selected risk management technique. Managerial decisions refer to how to work with others outside the risk management professional's direct authority to integrate risk management into the organization's procedures or production processes.

8-2. A risk management professional might make the following technical decisions in implementing a decision to insure a loss exposure:

- Select the appropriate insurer
- Set proper limits and deductibles
- Negotiate the purchase of the insurance

8-3. A risk management professional must work cooperatively with others in the organization to implement risk management techniques because risk management professionals are typically not subject to the line authority of the organization's management. The risk management professional must be alert to the organization's needs and the needs of other departments and employees to facilitate the integration of chosen techniques.

8-4. The CRO should work cooperatively with other managers because those managers already manage risk in their respective areas and the CRO may not have direct authority over those areas. For example, the CRO's responsibilities might have been expanded to include the organization's financial risk (credit risk, foreign exchange rate risk, and so forth), but these areas are directly controlled by others. In this instance, the CRO may find herself consulting with the managers in those areas rather than directing their activities.

Educational Objective 9

9-1. Activity and results standards may serve as a basis for monitoring the risk management program.

9-2. An organization's risk management program may need to be revised as a result of the following situations:

- Development of new loss exposures
- Increased significance of existing loss exposures
- Increased appropriateness of other risk management techniques

9-3. If a revision is required, an organization should repeat some or all of the six steps of the risk management process.

9-4. Department Store's risk management professionals may want to evaluate the use of insurance as a risk financing technique because of the increased cost of insurance.

Educational Objective 10

10-1. Three theoretical concepts that explain why ERM works are as follows:

   (1) Interdependency

   (2) Correlation

   (3) Portfolio theory

10-2. Uncorrelated risks check or counterbalance the effects of other risks' intrinsic volatility. This process is known as internal hedging.

10-3. Some of the sources of these problems include the following:

   • Reluctance to share trade secrets

   • Intradepartmental jargon

   • Manager's actions to defend their areas of responsibility from perceived attack

   • Lack of senior management's clearly articulated support for ERM

10-4. Because Large Pharmaceutical Company is a publicly traded company, the first driver may be to stay in compliance with SOX Section 404 and with regulations from the NYSE and SEC. In fact, some CEOs are concerned that without an ERM program in place, senior management will be unable to provide the necessary SOX certifications. Additionally, if Large Pharmaceutical Company relies on a financial rating from Standard and Poor's to help it negotiate its debt, an ERM program may favorably influence the rating agency to give it a higher rating than it would receive without such a program. So, achieving optimal financial ratings is a second driver to adopt ERM. A third driver is creating a competitive advantage, which Large Pharmaceutical may need to maintain its market share. One such advantage is enabling an organization to exploit opportunities not identified by competitors.

Direct Your Learning

Assessing Property Loss Exposures

Educational Objectives

After learning the content of this assignment, you should be able to:

1. Describe property exposed to loss.

2. Describe the major causes of loss affecting property.

3. Describe the methods of valuing property.

4. Describe the legal interests in property.

5. Describe the methods of identifying property loss exposures.

6. Define or describe each of the Key Words and Phrases for this assignment.

Study Materials

Required Reading:

▶ Risk Assessment
  • Chapter 3

Study Aids:

▶ SMART Online Practice Exams

▶ SMART Study Aids
  • Review Notes and Flash Cards— Assignment 3

Outline

▶ **Property Exposed to Loss**

A. Real Property
1. Land
2. Buildings and Other Structures

B. Personal Property
1. Tangible Personal Property
2. Intangible Personal Property

▶ **Major Causes of Loss Affecting Property**

A. Natural Causes of Loss
1. Windstorm
2. Earthquake
3. Flood
4. Fire and Lightning
5. Smoke
6. Hail
7. Weight of Snow, Sleet, and Ice
8. Water
9. Volcanic Action
10. Sinkhole Collapse

B. Human Causes of Loss
1. Riot and Civil Commotion
2. Explosion
3. Vandalism
4. Vehicles
5. Collapse
6. Aircraft
7. Crime
8. Falling Objects

C. Economic Causes of Loss

▶ **Methods of Valuing Property**

A. Historical Cost
B. Tax-Appraised Value
C. Book Value
D. Replacement Cost
1. Buildings
2. Personal Property
E. Reproduction Cost
F. Functional Replacement Cost
G. Market Value
H. Actual Cash Value
I. Economic Value

▶ **Legal Interests in Property**

A. Ownership Interest
B. Secured Creditor's Interest
C. Seller's and Buyer's Interest
D. Bailee's Interest
E. Landlord's Interest
F. Tenant's Interest

▶ **Methods of Identifying Property Loss Exposures**

A. Risk Assessment Questionnaires
B. Loss Histories
C. Financial Statements and Underlying Accounting Records
D. Other Records and Documents
E. Flowcharts
F. Personal Inspections
G. Expertise Within and Beyond the Organization

▶ **Summary**

Actively capture information by using the open space in the SMART Review Notes to write out key concepts. Putting information into your own words is an effective way to push that information into your memory.

For each assignment, you should define or describe each of the Key Words and Phrases and answer each of the Review and Application Questions.

Educational Objective 1
Describe property exposed to loss.

Key Words and Phrases
Unimproved land (p. 3.3)

Improved land (p. 3.4)

Computer virus (p. 3.7)

Copyright (p. 3.8)

Trademark (p. 3.9)

Patent (p. 3.9)

Trade secret (p. 3.9)

Goodwill (p. 3.9)

Review Questions

1-1.   Identify attributes of unimproved land that may make it difficult to value. (p. 3.4)

1-2.   Describe four attributes traditionally used to assess structures. (pp. 3.4–3.5)

1-3.   Identify the six construction categories used by Insurance Services Office (ISO). (p. 3.5)

1-4.   Describe the following categories of tangible property and the issues that a risk management professional needs to consider with each:

   a. Money and securities (p. 3.6)

   b. Accounts receivable records (p. 3.6)

▶▶

c. Inventory (p. 3.7)

d. Furniture, equipment, or supplies (p. 3.7)

e. Computer equipment and media (p. 3.7)

f. Machinery (pp. 3.7–3.8)

g. Valuable papers and records (p. 3.8)

h. Mobile property (p. 3.8)

Application Question

1-5. Langton, Inc., a running shoe manufacturer, has developed a
unique shoe design that improves runner speed while reducing
the endurance required to run. These shoes are aggressively
marketed by Langton and are easily recognizable because
of the Langton logo. What property might Langton's risk
management professional want to value? (pp. 3.8–3.9)

Educational Objective 2
Describe the major causes of loss affecting property.

Key Words and Phrases
Windstorm (p. 3.10)

Flood (p. 3.12)

Collapse (p. 3.21)

Review Questions

2-1. Describe the types of windstorms that can cause property loss.
(p. 3.10)

2-2.   Describe the two measures of earthquakes. (p. 3.12)

2-3.   Give examples of water sources that may cause water damage.
        (p. 3.19)

2-4.   Identify types of damage that typically result from rioting.
        (p. 3.20)

2-5.   Describe the two most common types of explosions. (p. 3.21)

Application Question

2-6. Major Retailer has locations throughout Florida and is subject to many of the causes of loss listed in Exhibit 3-1 of the text. Identify three causes of loss from Exhibit 3-1 to which Major Retailer may be susceptible.

Educational Objective 3
Describe the methods of valuing property.

Key Words and Phrases
Historical cost (p. 3.23)

Tax-appraised value (p. 3.24)

Book value (p. 3.24)

Replacement cost (p. 3.24)

Reproduction cost (p. 3.28)

Functional replacement cost (p. 3.29)

Market value (p. 3.29)

Actual cash value (p. 3.30)

Economic value (p. 3.30)

Review Questions

3-1.   Identify the approaches to valuing property. (p. 3.23)

3-2.   Explain the disadvantage of using the book value of a property from a risk management perspective. (p. 3.24)

3-3.   Explain the circumstances in which a risk management professional may choose reproduction cost as a means of valuing property. (p. 3.28)

3-4. Explain the circumstances in which a risk management professional may choose functional replacement cost as a means of valuing property. (p. 3.29)

3-5. Explain the circumstances in which a risk management professional may choose market value as a means of valuing property. (p. 3.29)

Application Question

3-6. Childrens' Hospital was built two years ago on property donated by a philanthropist. The former home of the philanthropist, a fifty-room mansion, is now part of the hospital and is used as offices. What approaches might the hospital's risk management professional use to value its property?

▶▶

Educational Objective 4
Describe the legal interests in property.

Key Words and Phrases
Secured creditor (p. 3.32)

Bailee (p. 3.32)

Bailor (p. 3.32)

Bailment contract (p. 3.32)

Improvements and betterments (p. 3.34)

Trade fixtures (p. 3.34)

Review Questions
4-1.   Identify the categories of legal interests in property. (p. 3.31)

4-2.   Describe two ways a common carrier's liability may be limited.
(p. 3.33)

4-3.   Describe the legal interests of tenants regarding the following:
(p. 3.34)

a. Improvements and betterments

b. Trade fixtures

Application Question

4-4.   Grocery Store operates its business from a building owned by
Leasing Company. Grocery Store has made numerous improvements to the building, including permanent walls that separate
the retail section of the store from the storage section of the
store. Grocery Store has also added merchandise shelves
(called gondolas) that form the aisles of the store. What
responsibility, if any, would Leasing Company have to Grocery Store for damages to Grocery Store's improvements? (pp.
3.33–3.34)

Educational Objective 5

Describe the methods of identifying property loss exposures.

Review Questions

5-1. Describe the methods used to identify property loss exposures. (pp. 3.34–3.38)

5-2. Explain why a risk management professional should not be dependant on loss histories alone to identify property loss exposures. (p. 3.35)

5-3. How might a risk management professional use an organization's financial statements and underlying accounting records to identify property loss exposures? (p. 3.36)

Application Question

5-4. Hadley Moving Company specializes in moving household
      goods anywhere in the United States. Hadley's employees enter
      the homes from which customers are moving, pack all or part
      of the household goods, load the belongings onto trucks that
      Hadley owns, drive the trucks to the customers' new homes,
      and unpack and place the household goods in the customers'
      new homes.

      When a customer whose belongings make up less than a full
      truckload is moving several hundred miles, the customer's
      property may be stored for a short period in one of thirty ware-
      houses that Hadley leases throughout the country until enough
      furniture from other customers makes up a full truckload going
      to the same city. When not in use, Hadley's vans are garaged
      and maintained in the nearest Hadley warehouse.

      Hadley maintains a small office in each of the warehouses.
      Customer records, through which local billings and customer
      payments are handled, are kept in these offices. Hadley's local
      offices exchange data with Hadley's main office.

      Construct a flowchart for Hadley's operations.

Answers to Assignment 3 Questions

NOTE: These answers are provided to give students a basic understanding of acceptable types of responses. They often are not the only valid answers and are not intended to provide an exhaustive response to the questions.

Educational Objective 1

1-1. Attributes of unimproved land that may make it difficult to value include water, mineral resources, natural attractions of commercial value, natural forests, or resident wild animals.

1-2. The four attributes traditionally used to assess structures are as follows:

    (1) Construction—how a structure is built

    (2) Occupancy—how a structure is used

    (3) Protection—risk control techniques used to prevent or reduce loss to the structure

    (4) External exposure—causes of loss that originate outside the structure

1-3. The six construction categories used by ISO are as follows:

    (1) Frame

    (2) Joisted masonry

    (3) Noncombustible

    (4) Masonry noncombustible

    (5) Modified fire resistive

    (6) Fire restive

1-4. The following are categories of tangible property and the issues that a risk management professional needs to consider with each:

    a. Money and securities—includes cash, bank accounts, certificates of deposit, securities, notes, drafts, and evidence of debt. The risk management professional needs to consider an organization's cash on hand, seasonal patterns, and possibility of theft.

    b. Accounts receivable records—records that show the money currently due and previously collected from customer or client accounts. The risk management professional needs to consider an organization's data backup and offsite storage.

    c. Inventory—includes goods ready for sale, raw materials, stock in process, and finished goods. The risk management professional needs to consider the fluctuating values at different production stages and the wide range of causes of loss.

    d. Furniture, equipment, or supplies—includes office furniture, showcases, counters, and office supplies. The risk management professional needs to consider the organization's ownership of supplies and of expensive or specialized equipment that cannot be easily replaced.

    e. Computer equipment and media—includes computers and other data-processing hardware, software, data, media, and specialized environmental control systems. The risk management professional needs to consider physical damage causes of loss, fraud, sabotage, theft of laptops, leased equipment, and obsolescence.

    f. Machinery—includes equipment and computer-controlled equipment. The risk management professional needs to consider the significant expense of this equipment.

g.   Valuable papers and records—includes medical histories of patients, project reference files, and physical documents associated with intangible property, such as deeds and films. The risk management professional needs to consider the organization's method of safekeeping and the valuation of valuable papers and records.

h.   Mobile property—includes autos, aircraft, boats, ships, and mobile equipment. The risk management professional needs to consider the large values of some items and the special hazards associated with them.

1-5.   Langton's risk management professional should be interested in the value of the unique shoe design and its logo. The unique shoe design is likely patented. Valuable rights are associated with that patent. However, exactly how valuable they are is the risk management professional's challenge. Langton's logo is likely trademarked. The logo enables consumers to readily identify its products over competitors, and therefore also has value.

Educational Objective 2

2-1.   The following types of windstorms can cause property loss:

- Hurricane—a severe tropical cyclone, usually accompanied by heavy rains and winds of seventy-five miles per hour or more.

- Tornado—a localized and violently destructive windstorm occurring over land and characterized by a funnel-shaped cloud extending toward the ground. A tornado consists of rotating winds at speeds up to 300 mph and upward velocity that can exceed 200 feet per second.

2-2.   The two measures of earthquakes are the Richter scale and the Modified Mercalli scale. The Richter scale measures the magnitude of an earthquake by the amount of energy released. The Modified Mercalli scale measures the intensity of an earthquake.

2-3.   Examples of water sources that may cause water damage include burst water pipes, sewer backup, and sprinkler leakage.

2-4.   Types of damage that typically result from rioting include fire, breakage, theft, looting, and vandalism.

2-5.   The two most common types of explosions are combustion explosions and pressure explosions. Combustion explosions are caused when flammable clouds (dust) ignite. Pressure explosions occur when a pressure vessel cannot contain its internal pressure and therefore bursts.

2-6.   Because Major Retailer has locations throughout Florida, it is susceptible to various natural causes of loss, such as hurricanes and sinkhole collapse. Additionally, Major Retailer is subject to human causes of loss, such as fire, theft, forgery, fraud, and shrinkage. Lastly, Major Retailer may be subjected to economic causes of loss, such as changes in consumer tastes.

Educational Objective 3

3-1.   The approaches to valuing property are as follows:

- Historical cost
- Tax-appraised value
- Book value
- Replacement cost

- Reproduction cost
- Functional replacement cost
- Market value
- Actual cash value
- Economic value

3-2. The disadvantage of using the book value of a property is that book value is calculated using depreciation. Therefore, a long-term asset's book value is lower than its market value.

3-3. A risk management professional may choose reproduction cost as a means of valuing property when the damaged real or personal property would need to be duplicated, such as the case with works of art and buildings with ornate features.

3-4. A risk management professional may choose functional replacement cost as a means of valuing property when the damaged real or personal property could be replaced with other property that, while not the same, performs similarly, such as the case with property that is easily affected by technological changes.

3-5. A risk management professional may choose market value as a means of valuing property when the damaged property is a commodity, such as grain or oil, that is traded on an organized exchange, and therefore has a daily market value.

3-6. Childrens' Hospital's risk management professional will likely choose to use several approaches to value its property. Because the hospital is only two years old, historical cost might be very accurate. As with historical cost, book value may offer a relevant value because of the hospital's newness. Replacement cost is likely the best approach, although it may take considerable research to determine. The fifty-room mansion would best be valued using reproduction cost. Functional replacement cost may be the best approach to valuing the hospital's personal property because much of it is technologically based. Likewise, market value may be appropriate for many items of the hospital's personal property. If the hospital has insured property for its actual cash value, it may be important to know the actual cash value so that a possible shortfall could be determined if the property were destroyed. Economic value may be a consideration for the hospital, but other property valuation methods would likely be more useful.

Educational Objective 4

4-1. The categories of legal interests in property are as follows:
- Ownership interest
- Secured creditor's interest
- Seller's and buyer's interest
- Bailee's interest
- Landlord's interest
- Tenant's interest

4-2. A common carrier's liability may be limited by statute or the common carrier's bill of lading (the contract between the parties). If liability is not limited, a common carrier is responsible for the full value of the property transported.

4-3. The legal interests of tenants are as follows:

    a. Improvements and betterments—alterations to the premises that are intended to remain permanently attached to the building and that make the property more useful for the tenant's purpose. These alternations become part of the leased structure.

    b. Trade fixtures—alterations to the premises that are not intended to remain permanently attached to the building. These alterations are usually treated as personal property and may be removed when the tenant leaves.

4-4. Leasing Company would not normally be responsible for the value of either (1) the improvements and betterments (that is, the wall separating the retail section of the store and the storage section of the store) or (2) the trade fixtures (that is, the gondolas). However, the lease between Leasing Company and Grocery Store may specify otherwise, and it would take precedence.

Educational Objective 5

5-1. The methods used to identify property loss exposures are as follows:

- Risk assessment questionnaires—questions designed to prompt risk management professionals to consider all of the organization's property loss exposures. Questionnaires often include extensive lists of property owned or leased.

- Loss histories—include types of past losses, their magnitude, and frequency.

- Financial statements and underlying accounting records—include an organization's balance sheet, income statement, and statement of cash flows.

- Other records and documents—include an organization's corporate charter, copyrights, trademarks, patents, architectural drawings, board or committee meeting minutes, and client records.

- Flowcharts—depict the productive sequence of activities.

- Personal inspections—include inspections of an organization's and its suppliers' premises and facilities.

- Expertise within and beyond the organization—include discussions with an organization's employees and with external experts such as property appraisers and technology experts.

5-2. A risk management professional should not depend on loss histories alone to identify property loss exposures because of the following issues:

- The organization may have disposed of property that suffered past losses or may have acquired new types of property with no loss records.

- Physical, managerial, and economic environments may have changed.

- Industry averages may not be relevant to the organization for which losses are being forecast.

- Historical data may understate frequency or severity of the type of property loss.

- Historical losses may not give reliable indications of property values.

5-3. A risk management professional might use an organization's financial statements and underlying accounting records to identify assets that contribute significantly to revenues. Assets involved in producing the largest segments of an organization's revenues are operationally the most important.

5-4.   A flowchart for Hadley's operations may look as follows:

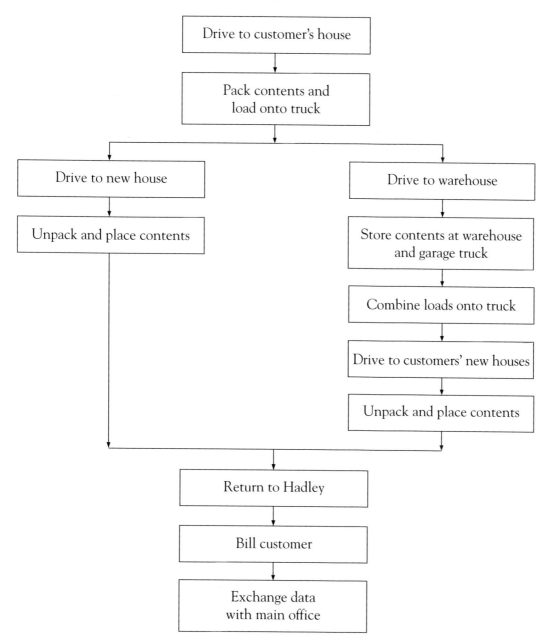

Direct Your Learning

Understanding the Legal Foundations of Liability Loss Exposures

Educational Objectives

After learning the content of this assignment, you should be able to:

1. Describe liability loss exposures arising out of torts.

2. Describe liability loss exposures arising out of contracts.

3. Describe liability loss exposures arising out of statutes.

4. Define or describe each of the Key Words and Phrases for this assignment.

Study Materials

Required Reading:
▶ Risk Assessment
  • Chapter 4

Study Aids:
▶ SMART Online Practice Exams
▶ SMART Study Aids
  • Review Notes and Flash Cards—Assignment 4

Outline

▶ **Legal Liability Based on Torts**

   A. Negligence

      1. Elements of Negligence

      2. Defenses to Negligence

      3. Additional Factors in Proving Negligence

   B. Intentional Torts

      1. Torts Against the Person

      2. Torts Involving Property

      3. Torts Involving Business

   C. Strict Liability

▶ **Legal Liability Based on Contracts**

   A. Elements of a Contract

      1. Agreement

      2. Consideration

      3. Capacity to Contract

      4. Legal Purpose

   B. Statute of Frauds

   C. Breach of Contract

   D. Hold-Harmless Agreements

▶ **Legal Liability Based on Statutes**

   A. Workers' Compensation Statutes

   B. Other Statutes Imposing Strict Liability

▶ **Summary**

Use the SMART Online Practice Exams to test your understanding of the course material. You can review questions over a single assignment or multiple assignments, or you can take an exam over the entire course. The questions are scored, and you are shown your results. (You score essay exams yourself.)

For each assignment, you should define or describe each of the Key Words and Phrases and answer each of the Review and Application Questions.

Educational Objective 1
Describe liability loss exposures arising out of torts.

Key Words and Phrases
Legal liability (p. 4.3)

Tort (p. 4.4)

Negligence (p. 4.4)

Common law (p. 4.5)

Statute (p. 4.5)

Proximate cause (p. 4.6)

Compensatory damages (p. 4.7)

Special damages (p. 4.7)

General damages (p. 4.7)

Punitive damages (p. 4.7)

Injunction (p. 4.8)

Contributory negligence (p. 4.8)

Comparative negligence (p. 4.9)

Assumption of risk (p. 4.10)

Statute of limitations (p. 4.10)

Negligence per se (p. 4.11)

Joint and several liability (p. 4.11)

Res ipsa loquitur (p. 4.12)

Vicarious liability (p. 4.12)

Intentional tort (p. 4.13)

Assault (p. 4.14)

Battery (p. 4.14)

False imprisonment (p. 4.14)

False arrest (p. 4.14)

Defamation (p. 4.14)

Libel (p. 4.14)

Slander (p. 4.14)

Malicious prosecution (p. 4.15)

Malicious abuse of process (p. 4.15)

Trespass (p. 4.15)

Conversion (p. 4.15)

Nuisance (p. 4.16)

Fraud (p. 4.16)

Trade disparagement (p. 4.17)

Strict liability, or absolute liability (p. 4.17)

Review Questions

1-1. Identify the three main bases of legal liability. (p. 4.3)

▶▶

1-2. Distinguish between civil law and criminal law. (p. 4.4)

1-3. Describe the three broad types of torts. (pp. 4.4, 4.13, 4.17)

1-4. Identify the four elements of negligence. (p. 4.5)

1-5. When the common law and statutes conflict, which takes precedence? (p. 4.5)

1-6. Identify the two broad categories of damages that a plaintiff can recover under tort law. (p. 4.6)

1-7.   Identify the two types of compensatory damages a plaintiff may
       be able to recover if negligence is successfully proved. (p. 4.7)

1-8.   Describe defenses a defendant may use to rebut a plaintiff's
       allegation of negligence. (pp. 4.8–4.10)

1-9.   What is the intention behind statutes of limitations? (p. 4.10)

1-10. Describe the circumstances in which negligence per se may be
       successfully used by a plaintiff. (p. 4.11)

1-11. What conditions must be satisfied for a plaintiff to successfully
       use the *res ipsa loquitur* doctrine in a lawsuit? (p. 4.12)

1-12. How is an intentional tort distinguished from negligence? (p. 4.13)

1-13. Provide examples of intentional torts against the person. (p. 4.14)

1-14. Identify the two forms that defamation may take. (p. 4.14)

1-15. Identify four common-law situations that are examples of invasion of privacy. (p. 4.14)

1-16. Identify the elements of tort liability for fraud. (pp. 4.16–4.17)

1-17. Identify two situations in which strict liability in tort is imposed by tort law. (p. 4.17)

Application Questions

1-18. Shopper slipped on a wet floor in the produce section of Supermarket and brings a claim against Supermarket. Supermarket contests liability, and the lawsuit goes to court.

    a. What must Shopper prove?

    b. What defenses might Supermarket use?

    c. If Shopper lost wages because of this incident, which type of damages could be recoverable?

1-19. Patient discovers that a pair of forceps is in his body. The only surgical procedure Patient has had was to remove his gallbladder five years ago. How might Patient prove negligence against Doctor? (p. 4.12)

1-20. Store Security "arrests" Customer in front of Store's jewelry counter. Store Security shouts, "I've seen you shoplifting ten times before, but now I have caught you red-handed." Store Security handcuffs Customer and holds her in a detention room for three hours until the local police can arrive. Store Security searches Customer's purse and finds only the watch that she had brought to Store for a new battery. Identify, if any, the intentional torts Store may be accused of committing. (p. 4.14)

Educational Objective 2

Describe liability loss exposures arising out of contracts.

Key Words and Phrases

Offer (p. 4.18)

Acceptance (p. 4.18)

Unilateral contract (p. 4.20)

Bilateral contract (p. 4.20)

Consideration (p. 4.20)

Competence (p. 4.21)

Capacity to contract (p. 4.21)

Statute of frauds (p. 4.21)

Breach of contract (p. 4.22)

Review Questions

2-1.   Identify the ways legal liability based on contracts can arise.
        (p. 4.18)

▶▶

2-2. Identify the four elements that must be present to create a legally enforceable contract. (p. 4.18)

2-3. Identify the requirements of a contractual offer. (p. 4.19)

2-4. Identify the requirements of a contractual acceptance. (p. 4.20)

2-5. Identify consideration that might be necessary to make a contract enforceable. (p. 4.20)

2-6. Describe the four categories of damages recoverable for a breach of contract. (p. 4.22)

Application Question

2-7. Snowplow Operator clears one foot of snow from the parking lot of Executive Business Complex without being asked. Snowplow Operator submits an invoice, and Executive Business Complex refuses to pay. Explain the elements of a contract that may be missing.

Educational Objective 3

Describe liability loss exposures arising out of statutes.

Review Questions

3-1. What is the basic purpose of all workers' compensation statutes? (p. 4.24)

3-2. Identify the benefits provided to an injured or ill employee by workers' compensation statutes. (p. 4.24)

3-3. What is required for an employee to collect workers' compensation benefits? (p. 4.24)

3-4. Other than workers' compensation laws, identify another situation in which a statute imposes strict liability. (p. 4.24)

Application Question

3-5. During a slow period, two warehouse workers used their forklifts to joust with one another. One of the workers was injured. What compensation, if any, does the employer owe the injured worker? (p. 4.24)

Answers to Assignment 4 Questions

NOTE: These answers are provided to give students a basic understanding of acceptable types of responses. They often are not the only valid answers and are not intended to provide an exhaustive response to the questions.

Educational Objective 1

1-1. The three main bases of legal liability are (1) torts, (2) contacts, and (3) statutes.

1-2. Civil law applies to legal matters not governed by criminal law. Criminal law applies to acts that society deems so harmful to the public welfare that government takes the responsibility for prosecuting and punishing perpetrators.

1-3. The three broad types of torts are as follows:

   (1) Negligence—the failure to exercise the degree of care that a reasonably prudent person would have exercised under similar circumstances to avoid harming another person or legal entity

   (2) Intentional torts—acts committed with general or specific intent to perform a harmful act that is held to be a tort

   (3) Strict liability torts—acts committed with neither negligence nor intent to harm

1-4. The four elements of negligence are as follows:

   (1) The defendant owed a legal duty of care to the plaintiff.

   (2) The defendant breached the duty of care owed to the plaintiff.

   (3) The defendant's breach of duty was the proximate cause of the plaintiff's injury or damage.

   (4) The plaintiff suffered actual injury or damage.

1-5. Statutes (and ordinances) can alter or amend common-law duties and therefore take precedence.

1-6. The two broad categories of damages that a plaintiff can recover under tort law are as follows:

   (1) Compensatory damages, which compensate the plaintiff

   (2) Punitive damages, which punish the defendant

1-7. The two types of compensatory damages a plaintiff may be able to recover if negligence is successfully proved are as follows:

   (1) Special damages—compensatory damages for actual losses that can include the cost to repair or replace damaged property, costs resulting from the loss of use of damaged property, loss of earnings resulting from the death or disability of the plaintiff, and reasonable medical expenses incurred by the plaintiff.

   (2) General damages—compensatory damages that include compensation for pain and suffering, mental anguish, bereavement from the death of a loved one, and the loss of the consortium of a deceased or disabled spouse.

1-8. Defenses a defendant may use to rebut a plaintiff's allegation of negligence include the following:

   • Contributory negligence—the plaintiff's own negligence in part caused the plaintiff's harm; therefore, the plaintiff is prevented from recovering damages.

   • Comparative negligence—the plaintiff's negligence in part caused the plaintiff's harm, and consequently the plaintiff's recovery from the defendant is reduced proportionately.

- Assumption of risk—the plaintiff knowingly and voluntarily accepted the possibility of harm and therefore cannot later seek damages from a negligent defendant.
- Statute of limitations—the plaintiff is prevented from suing the defendant after the expiration of the time set forth in the statute of limitations.
- Immunities—the plaintiff is prevented from suing a defendant organization that is protected by an immunity.

1-9. The intention behind statutes of limitations is that there should be some point at which the threat of litigation must cease.

1-10. A plaintiff may be able to successfully use negligence per se when the defendant's act is considered inherently negligent because the defendant violated a law or an ordinance.

1-11. A plaintiff must satisfy the following conditions to successfully use the *res ipsa loquitur* doctrine in a lawsuit:
- The cause of the accident was within the defendant's exclusive control.
- The accident was one that would not happen in the ordinary course of events.
- The accident was not the result of the plaintiff's own negligence.

1-12. An intentional tort is a tort committed with general or specific intent to perform the act that is held to be a tort. Negligence is an unintentional tort.

1-13. The following are examples of intentional torts against the person:
- Assault
- Battery
- False imprisonment
- False arrest
- Defamation
- Invasion of privacy
- Malicious prosecution
- Malicious abuse of process

1-14. Defamation can take the following two forms:
(1) Libel—a defamatory statement expressed in a written or fixed form
(2) Slander—a defamatory statement expressed by speech

1-15. Four common-law situations that are examples of invasion of privacy are: (1) intrusion on solitude or seclusion, (2) physical invasion, (3) public disclosure of private facts, and (4) unauthorized release of confidential information.

1-16. The elements of tort liability for fraud are as follows:
- A false representation—a true representation made maliciously is not fraud.
- Of a material fact—the misrepresentation must be material (important) and concern a past or an existing fact.
- Knowingly made—the defendant must know that the representation is false, or have reckless disregard as to whether the misrepresentation is false.

- With intent to deceive—the defendant must intend for the plaintiff to rely only on the misrepresentation.

- On which the other part has placed justifiable reliance—the plaintiff must actually and reasonably rely on the misrepresentation.

- To his or her detriment—the plaintiff must suffer actual damage.

1-17. Two situations in which strict liability in tort is imposed by tort law are (1) abnormally dangerous activities and (2) the sale of dangerously defective products.

1-18. In the Supermarket liability case, the following points apply:

a. Shopper must prove that Supermarket was negligent. To prove negligence, Shopper must prove all of the following: (1) Supermarket owed a legal duty of care to Shopper, (2) Supermarket breached the legal duty of care owed to Shopper, (3) the wet floor was the proximate cause of Shopper's fall, and (4) Shopper sustained actual injury or property damage.

b. Supermarket might defend this lawsuit by asserting that the elements of negligence are not present. For example, Supermarket might present evidence that Shopper was not injured by the fall. In addition to elements of negligence, Supermarket might raise the following defenses: (1) contributory negligence, (2) comparative negligence, (3) assumption of risk, or (4) statute of limitations. For example, Supermarket might have video surveillance that shows Shopper purposely sliding across the wet floor as an antic.

c. Shopper's lost wages are included in the category of special damages and could be recovered if negligence is proved.

1-19. Patient would likely use the legal doctrine *res ipsa loquitur* in pursuing the lawsuit against Doctor. This approach is appropriate because negligence can be inferred by the discovery of the forceps.

1-20. Store Security may be accused of committing all of the following intentional torts:

- Assault—Store Security might have used threat of force on Shopper.

- Battery—handcuffing Shopper might be considered harmful or offensive contact.

- False imprisonment—holding Shopper for three hours without Shopper's consent.

- False arrest—Shopper's forcible restraint.

- Slander—Store Security's shouting that Shopper is a shoplifter.

Educational Objective 2

2-1. Legal liability based on contracts can arise out of breach of contract or an agreement to assume the liability of another party (hold-harmless agreement).

2-2. The four elements that must be present to create a legally enforceable contract are: (1) agreement, (2) consideration, (3) capacity to contract, and (4) legal purpose.

2-3. The requirements of a contractual offer are the intent to contract, definite terms, and communication to offeree.

2-4. The requirements of a contractual acceptance are that the offeree must make the acceptance, the acceptance must be unconditional and unequivocal, and the offeree must communicate the acceptance to the offeror by appropriate word or act.

2-5. Consideration necessary to make a contract enforceable might consist of a return promise, an act performed, or a promise not to act.

2-6. The four categories of damages recoverable for a breach of contract are as follows:

(1) Compensatory damages—money that will offset the loss sustained

(2) Consequential damages—money awarded when the professional, at the time of contracting, was aware of some special or unusual circumstances that might occur as a result of the breach

(3) Liquidated damages—a specified dollar amount stipulated in the contract as the amount to be recovered if a breach occurs

(4) Nominal damages—small amounts awarded to a plaintiff when a wrong occurs but there is no compensable injury

2-7. Snowplow Operator failed to obtain an agreement with Executive Business Complex. Lacking this element, there is not an enforceable contract.

Educational Objective 3

3-1. The basic purpose of all workers' compensation statutes is to provide prompt compensation to injured employees without the need for a lawsuit.

3-2. The benefits provided to an injured or ill employee by workers' compensation statutes include medical expenses, income lost because of partial or total disability, rehabilitation services, and burial allowance and survivor benefits payable to the employee's spouse and dependent children.

3-3. To collect workers' compensation benefits, an employee needs to establish coverage by the relevant workers' compensation law and establish that the injury arose out of and in the course of employment.

3-4. Some states have statutes that make every auto owner legally liable for negligent operation of the auto by anyone who operates the auto with the owner's permission.

3-5. The injured worker's employer must provide workers' compensation benefits to the injured worker despite the worker's role in his own injury.

Direct Your Learning

Assessing Liability Loss Exposures, Part I

Educational Objectives

After learning the content of this assignment, you should be able to:

1. Explain how liability loss exposures arise out of premises and operations.

    - Describe the basis for liability arising out of premises and operations, including the duty owed to the following:

        - Business invitees

        - Licensees

        - Trespassers

    - Describe the liability loss exposures arising out of slip-and-fall in ice and snow.

    - Describe the liability loss exposures arising out of premises security.

    - Describe the liability loss exposures arising out of mobile equipment.

    - Describe the liability loss exposures arising out of liquor liability.

    - Describe the liability loss exposures arising out of bailment.

2. Explain how products liability arises out of the following:

    - Breach of warranty

    - Negligence

    - Strict liability in tort

3. Describe the defenses to products liability.

4. Describe the liability loss exposures arising out of completed operations.

5. Describe the liability loss exposures arising out of the ownership, maintenance, or use of automobiles.

6. Identify the liability loss exposures faced by watercraft owners and operators.

7. Define or describe each of the Key Words and Phrases for this assignment.

Study Materials

Required Reading:
- Risk Assessment
  - Chapter 5

Study Aids:
- SMART Online Practice Exams
- SMART Study Aids
  - Review Notes and Flash Cards—Assignment 5

Outline

▶ **Premises and Operations Liability Loss Exposures**

A. Basis for Premises and Operations Liability

1. Legal Duty Owed

2. Breach of the Legal Duty Owed

3. Proximate Cause

4. Damages and Other Remedies

B. Slip-and-Fall in Ice and Snow Liability

C. Premises Security Liability

1. Liability for Crimes Committed by Employees

2. Liability for Criminal Attacks Committed by Third Parties

D. Mobile Equipment Liability

E. Liquor Liability

1. Dram Shop and Liquor Control Statutes

2. Employer Hosts

3. Social Hosts

4. Common-Law Defenses to Liquor Liability

F. Bailment Liability

1. Types of Bailments

2. Defenses and Limitations on Bailment Liability

▶ **Products Liability Loss Exposures**

A. Breach of Warranty

B. Negligence

C. Strict Liability in Tort

1. Who May Bring an Action?

2. Elements of Strict Liability in Tort

D. Defenses to Products Liability

1. State of the Art

2. Compliance With Product Specifications

3. Open and Obvious Danger

4. Plaintiff's Knowledge

5. Contributory or Comparative Negligence and Assumption of Risk

6. Product Misuse

7. Product Alteration

8. Written Disclaimers

9. Post-Accident Product Changes

10. Existence of an Intermediary

11. Allergy and Susceptibility

▶ **Completed Operations Liability Loss Exposures**

▶ **Automobile Liability Loss Exposures**

A. Liability for Operation by Others

1. Employer-Employee

2. Volunteers

3. Loaned Employees

B. Auto No-Fault Statutes

▶ **Watercraft Liability Loss Exposures**

A. Liability Loss Exposures for Bodily Injury

B. Liability Loss Exposures for Property Damage

C. Liability for Pollution

▶ **Summary**

The SMART Online Practice Exams product contains a final practice exam. You should take this exam only when you have completed your study of the entire course. Take this exam under simulated exam conditions. It will be your best indicator of how well prepared you are.

For each assignment, you should define or describe each of the Key Words and Phrases and answer each of the Review and Application Questions.

Educational Objective 1

Explain how liability loss exposures arise out of premises and operations.

- Describe the basis for liability arising out of premises and operations, including the duty owed to:
  - Business invitees
  - Licensees
  - Trespassers
- Describe the liability loss exposures arising out of slip-and-fall in ice and snow.
- Describe the liability loss exposures arising out of premises security.
- Describe the liability loss exposures arising out of mobile equipment.
- Describe the liability loss exposures arising out of liquor liability.
- Describe the liability loss exposures arising out of bailment.

Key Words and Phrases

Business invitee (p. 5.5)

Actual notice (p. 5.5)

Constructive notice (p. 5.5)

Licensee (p. 5.6)

Trespasser (p. 5.6)

Attractive nuisance (p. 5.6)

Review Questions

1-1.   Identify the legal duty owed by a property owner or occupier to the following categories of individuals: (pp. 5.5–5.6)

    a. Business invitees

    b. Licensees

    c. Trespassers

1-2.   Provide two examples of activities that would negate the duty of care owed to a business invitee. (p. 5.6)

1-3. Identify the elements of evidence necessary to establish liability under the attractive nuisance doctrine. (pp. 5.6–5.7)

1-4. Identify four factors related to foreseeability that are used by courts in evaluating a property owner's or an occupier's liability. (p. 5.8)

1-5. Identify possible defenses for a liability claim resulting from a slip-and-fall in ice and snow. (p. 5.11)

1-6. Identify the four legal principles on which liability for criminal attacks committed by third parties is based. (p. 5.12)

1-7. Identify moveable equipment that could be a source of mobile equipment liability for an organization. (p. 5.13)

1-8.   Identify commonly used bases for recovery in liquor liability
cases. (p. 5.13)

1-9.   To whom do dram shop statutes apply? (p. 5.15)

1-10. Describe the application of dram shop laws in cases involving
the following: (pp. 5.14–5.15)

a. Employer hosts

b. Social hosts

1-11. Identify the three classes of bailments and the degree of care
that a bailee must exercise. (p. 5.15)

1-12. Describe bailee liability for a customer's property for the following types of bailees: (p. 5.17)

　　a. Innkeepers (hotels and motels)

　　b. Storekeepers

　　c. Restaurateurs

　　d. Common carriers

Application Questions

1-13. Discuss preventative actions that might be taken by a garden store retailer to decrease the possibility of liability exposures.

1-14. Identify two examples of losses that might be caused by a garden store retailer using mobile equipment.

Educational Objective 2

Explain how products liability arises out of the following:

- **Breach of warranty**
- **Negligence**
- **Strict liability in tort**

Key Words and Phrases

Breach of warranty (p. 5.18)

Implied warranty (p. 5.18)

Implied warranty of merchantability (p. 5.19)

Implied warranty of fitness for purpose (p. 5.19)

Express warranty (p. 5.19)

Privity of contract (p. 5.21)

Review Questions

2-1. List three sources of products liability claims. (p. 5.18)

2-2. Identify the two implied warranties recognized by common law
and the Uniform Commercial Code. (pp. 5.18–5.19)

2-3. Identify the steps in a product's production process where
opportunities for negligence might occur. (p. 5.20)

Application Question

2-4.   Sunglasses Manufacturer develops a revolutionary lens coating that both blocks the elements of light that are harmful to the eyes and enhances the visual clarity of the wearer. Long-term wearers of these sunglasses file suit for bodily injury, claiming that the chemical coating causes eye irritation. What must the plaintiffs prove in a strict liability in tort action? (p. 5.23)

Educational Objective 3

Describe the defenses to products liability.

Review Questions

3-1.   Explain what is meant by "state of the art." (pp. 5.25–5.26)

3-2.   Identify possible defenses to products liability that might defeat a claim or reduce the amount of damages. (pp. 5.25–5.29)

3-3. Describe how the existence of an intermediary might affect a manufacturer's liability in a products liability case. (p. 5.28)

Application Question

3-4. Auto Parts Manufacturer builds power steering units for cars based on specifications provided by its customer, an automobile manufacturer. Car fires have been traced to the power steering units. What products liability defenses might Auto Parts Manufacturer assert if confronted by a claim resulting from the consequence of the car fires?

Educational Objective 4

Describe the liability loss exposures arising out of completed operations.

Review Questions

4-1. Describe completed operations liability. (p. 5.29)

4-2. Explain how a contractor's negligent installation of a boiler might lead to a completed operations liability loss for the contractor. (p. 5.29)

4-3. Explain how a contractor might face a completed operations liability loss from the sudden collapse of a homeowner's recently completed deck caused by the use of defective parts or materials. (p. 5.29)

Application Question

4-4. Which of the following are considered to be a completed operation loss exposure? (p. 5.29)

a. Plumber fails to properly vent the gas hot water heater, and members of the household succumb to carbon monoxide poisoning.

b. Small Engine Repairer fails to replace the pin holding on the propeller of an outboard motor, and the engine is damaged as a consequence.

c. Carpet Cleaner fails to notice a hose connection has come undone, and water consequently floods a customer's kitchen while the carpets are being cleaned.

d. Coffee Pot Manufacturer uses a faulty fuse in the power cord of its product, and its coffee pots are more likely to catch fire as a consequence.

Educational Objective 5

Describe the liability loss exposures arising out of the ownership, maintenance, or use of automobiles.

Review Questions

5-1. Give examples of commercial auto use, other than their operation on highways, that may create a liability loss exposure. (p. 5.31)

5-2. Describe three relationships that may give rise to an automobile liability loss exposure for operation of an auto by others. (pp. 5.31–5.32)

5-3. Describe two types of thresholds typically used in a no-fault system to determine the injured party's right to sue under auto no-fault statutes. (p. 5.32)

Application Question

5-4. Pizza Delivery hires college-age drivers to deliver pizzas in their personal vehicles. To what extent, if any, would Pizza Delivery be held responsible for claims from third parties in the following situations:

a. A Pizza Delivery driver runs a red light while hurrying to deliver pizzas, and strikes another vehicle.

b. A Pizza Delivery driver sideswipes a parked vehicle while on his way to work.

Educational Objective 6

Identify the liability loss exposures faced by watercraft owners and operators.

Review Questions

6-1. Identify three major loss exposures faced by watercraft owners
and operators. (p. 5.33)

6-2. Explain when general average losses occur and why the
expenses are considered a liability loss exposure. (p. 5.33)

6-3. Identify the possible liability loss exposures for property damage
that a vessel's owner might face after a collision with another
vessel. (p. 5.34)

Application Question

6-4.   Cargo Vessel becomes stranded on a sandbar, and the captain decides to jettison cargo to refloat the vessel. The jettisoned cargo belongs to one of four shippers with cargo on the ship and is valued at $250,000. With whom, if anyone, and for how much, if anything, will the loss of cargo be shared?

Answers to Assignment 5 Questions

NOTE: These answers are provided to give students a basic understanding of acceptable types of responses. They often are not the only valid answers and are not intended to provide an exhaustive response to the questions.

Educational Objective 1

1-1. The following are the legal duties owed by a property owner or occupier to the respective categories of individuals:

  a. Business invitees—the law requires that the owners or occupiers of a property take reasonable care to provide a safe premises for individuals on the property to conduct business and to make a reasonable effort to discover and correct hazardous conditions.

  b. Licensees—the law requires that the owners or occupiers of the property exercise the same degree of care as that imposed for ordinary negligence to individuals who have permission to be on the property, but are there for their own purpose.

  c. Trespassers—the law requires that the owners or occupiers of the property not intentionally harm or set traps for individuals who do not have the legal right to be on the premises.

1-2. Two examples of activities that would negate the duty of care owed to a business invitee are entering an area not open to the public (individual becomes a trespasser) and engaging in criminal activity, such as shoplifting.

1-3. The elements of evidence necessary to establish liability under the attractive nuisance doctrine are as follows:

  • The property owner or occupier knows or has reason to know that the attractive object is in an area where children are likely to trespass.

  • The property owner or occupier knows or has reason to know that the attractive object poses a serious risk to children.

  • The children who trespass are too young to understand the danger posed by the attractive object.

  • The object's benefit to the owner or occupier is slight compared to the risk it poses to the children.

  • The property owner or occupier fails to use reasonable care to eliminate the danger or protect the children.

1-4. The four factors related to foreseeability that are used by courts in evaluating a property owner's or occupier's liability are as follows:

  (1) What is the probability that harm would occur from the property owner's or occupier's actions (or failure to take action)?

  (2) How serious would the harm likely be?

  (3) What precautions could the property owner or occupier have taken to prevent harm?

  (4) How burdensome would the precautions have been to the property owner or occupier?

1-5. Possible defenses for a liability claim resulting from a slip-and-fall in ice and snow are as follows:

  • The ice and snow was a general condition of the community, and the hazards on the owner's or occupier's premises were no worse than those in any other area in the community at the time.

  • The owner or occupier made every reasonable effort to remove the ice or snow.

1-6. The four legal principles on which liability for criminal attacks committed by third parties is based are as follows:

(1) The property owner or occupier had a special relationship with the claimant that required offering a higher level of security.

(2) The property owner or occupier voluntarily assumed liability for the claimant's safety.

(3) The property owner or occupier violated a statute requiring certain security measures.

(4) Special circumstances existed that would made criminal attacks more likely so that the property owner or occupier should have foreseen and tried to prevent a particular attack.

1-7. Moveable equipment that could be a source of mobile equipment liability for an organization might include the following:

- Grounds equipment, such as forklifts, lawnmowers, and snow removal equipment

- Maintenance equipment, such as large vacuum cleaners, carpet cleaners, and buffers

- Heavy equipment, such as bulldozers, backhoes, and cherry pickers

1-8. Commonly used bases for recovery in liquor liability cases include dram shop statutes, liquor control statutes, or common-law negligence governing employer hosts and social hosts.

1-9. Dram shop statutes apply to owners or lessees of the property, bar, restaurant, or liquor store that serves alcoholic beverages.

1-10. Dram shop laws apply in the following manner:

a. Employer hosts—generally, the laws do not apply to employers serving alcohol to employees, but employers can still become liable because of the employer-employee relationship.

b. Social hosts—generally, social hosts are not held to the same degree of responsibility for the acts of their guests as those serving liquor for a profit. However, a social host who serves alcoholic drinks to an obviously intoxicated guest and who knows that the person would soon be driving may be held liable for resulting injury caused by the guest's drunken driving. Courts are usually more strict with hosts who serve liquor to minors.

1-11. The three classes of bailments and the degree of care a bailee must exercise are as follows:

(1) Bailments for the sole benefit of the bailor—the bailee must exercise slight care.

(2) Bailments for the sole benefit of the bailee—the bailee must exercise a high degree of care.

(3) Bailments for the mutual benefit of both parties—the bailee must exercise an ordinary degree of care.

1-12. Bailee liability for a customer's property can be described as follows:

a. Innkeepers (hotels and motels)—liability for guests' property is typically limited, particularly if safes are provided. Innkeepers are also relieved of bailee liability for acts of God, acts of war, or losses caused by guests' negligence.

b. Storekeepers—ordinarily responsible for a customer's clothing removed while temporarily trying on new clothes.

c. Restaurants—responsible for customers' property if a checkroom is available but not visually liable when property is placed on hooks or racks close to a customer's seat.

d. Common carriers—usually responsible for loss or damage to goods in their custody except for those resulting from acts of God, acts of war, acts of public authorities, inherent vice, or neglect by the shipper.

1-13. Preventive actions that might be taken by a garden store retailer to decrease the possibility of liability exposures include the following:

- Fence decorative pond area to prevent access by children
- Display insecticides safely and post warning of hazards
- Provide assistance to customers in lifting heavy items and delivering them to the customer's automobile
- Use gates prohibiting entrance into lot when business is closed
- Post "employees only" signs in off-limit areas
- Provide clear and well-marked paths throughout display area
- Conduct a pre-employment screening of staff

1-14. Two examples of losses that might be caused by a garden store retailer using mobile equipment are as follows:

(1) Injury to customers resulting from careless operation of forklift

(2) Damage to customers' autos caused by debris propelled by lawnmower

Educational Objective 2

2-1. Three sources of products liability claims are as follows:

(1) Breach of warranty

(2) Negligence

(3) Strict liability in tort

2-2. The two implied warranties recognized by common law and the Uniform Commercial Code are as follows:

(1) Implied warranty of merchantability

(2) Implied warranty of fitness for purpose

2-3. The steps in a product's production process that provide opportunities for negligence include the following:

- Product design
- Product manufacture
- Product inspection
- Product instructions and warnings

2-4. The plaintiffs must prove the following in a strict liability in tort action against Sunglasses Manufacturer:

- The product left Sunglasses Manufacturer's custody or control in a defective condition.
- The defective condition made the product unreasonably dangerous.
- The defective product was the proximate cause of the plaintiffs' injury.

Educational Objective 3

3-1.   "State of the art" means that the product conforms to industry customs and practices and to the technological feasibility of producing safer products based on scientific knowledge at the time.

3-2.   The following are possible defenses to products liability that might defeat the claim or reduce the amount of damages:

- State of the art
- Compliance with product specifications
- Open and obvious danger
- Plaintiff's knowledge
- Contributory or comparative negligence and assumption of risk
- Product misuse
- Product alteration
- Written disclaimers
- Post-accident product changes
- Existence of an intermediary
- Allergy and susceptibility

3-3.   If the manufacturer is held liable for a defect, the existence of an intermediary would not necessarily relieve the manufacturer's liability. However, the manufacturer will generally not be held liable if the intermediary's acts or omissions are the cause of the product defect and were not foreseeable. Similarly, if the manufacturer believes that the intermediary has taken steps to remove a defect or prevent danger, the manufacturer will not be held liable.

3-4.   Auto Parts Manufacturer would most likely assert the defense that the power steering unit it manufactured complied with the product specifications of the automobile manufacturer, and that any claim against it would be more appropriately directed at the automobile manufacturer.

Educational Objective 4

4-1.   Completed operations liability is the legal responsibility of a contractor, repairer, or other entity for bodily injury or property damage (real or personal) arising out of completed work, including defective parts or materials furnished with the work.

4-2.   If the negligent installation of the boiler resulted in an explosion, the contractor might be liable to the building's owner for property damage and to the tenant if injuries resulted from the explosion.

4-3.   If the homeowner or guests are injured because of a deck collapse caused by defective parts or materials furnished with the work, injured guests could sue the decking contractor for damages.

4-4.   a.   Plumber is considered to have a completed operations loss exposure.

b.   Small Engine Repair is considered to have a completed operations loss exposure.

c.   Carpet Cleaner is not considered to have a completed operations loss exposure. This would be considered to be a premises and operations loss exposure.

d.   Coffee Pot Manufacturer is not considered to have a completed operations loss exposure. This would be considered a products loss exposure.

Educational Objective 5

5-1. Examples of liability arising from the use of commercial autos, other than their operation on highways, include the following:

- Loading and unloading
- Use of the auto's trailer as a portable office, warehouse, store, library, museum, or clinic, or as a cage for animals or livestock
- Use with mounted equipment, such as well-digging equipment or a concrete mixer

5-2. Three relationships that may give rise to an automobile liability loss exposure for operation of an auto by others are as follows:

(1) Employer-employee—the employer may be vicariously liable for injuries and damage that result from negligent actions of employees while using automobiles within the scope of their employment.

(2) Volunteers—organizations that direct and control volunteers' activities may be responsible for the volunteers' negligence while operating automobiles within the scope of their activities.

(3) Loaned employees—responsibility for a loaned employee's negligent operation of automobiles depends on the loan arrangement; however, the greater the lessee's control, the greater likelihood that the lessee will be held liable.

5-3. Two types of thresholds typically used under auto no-fault statutes to determine the injured party's right to sue are as follows:

(1) Verbal thresholds—typically an injury that results in whole or partial loss of a body member or function, permanent disability or disfigurement, or death

(2) Monetary thresholds—A dollar limit in total medical expenses that an injured victim must exceed before he or she is permitted to sue the other party

5-4. a. Pizza Delivery will likely be held jointly liable for claims from third parties because the driver was acting within the scope of employment.

b. Pizza Delivery will likely assert that the driver's negligence did not occur during the course of employment and consequentially Pizza Delivery should not be held jointly liable in this instance.

Educational Objective 6

6-1. Three major loss exposures faced by watercraft owners and operators are as follows:

(1) Bodily injury, illness, or death of crew, shore workers, passengers, and persons not on board

(2) Property damage to, and loss of use of, vessels, cargo, bridges and other structures, and cargo or property of others

(3) Liability for pollution

6-2. General average losses occur when cargo is jettisoned to save a ship from sinking. The expenses are considered a liability loss exposure because the vessel owner (or cargo owner) can become legally obligated to pay others' losses or expenditures resulting from the action.

6-3. Possible liability loss exposures for property damage that a vessel's owner might face after a collision with another vessel include the following:
- Damage to the other vessel
- Wreck removal expenses
- Loss of the vessel's use
- Loss of freight
- Damage to the other vessel's cargo or other property
- Structures located on or near the water
- Damage to customers' cargo on board

6-4. Each of the four shippers and the vessel owner would share proportionately in the $250,000 loss; that is, $50,000 each.

Direct Your Learning

Assessing Liability Loss Exposures, Part II

Educational Objectives

After learning the content of this assignment, you should be able to:

1. Describe the liability loss exposures arising out of workers' compensation.

2. Describe the liability loss exposures arising out of environmental pollution.

3. Describe the liability loss exposures arising out of professional activities, including physicians, accountants, insurance agents and brokers, and architects and engineers.

4. Define or describe each of the Key Words and Phrases for this assignment.

Study Materials

Required Reading:
▶ Risk Assessment
  • Chapter 6

Study Aids:
▶ SMART Online Practice Exams
▶ SMART Study Aids
  • Review Notes and Flash Cards—Assignment 6

Outline

- ▶ **Workers' Compensation Liability Loss Exposures**
    - A. Employers' Liability Under Common Law
        - 1. Employers' Duty of Care
        - 2. Common-Law Defenses
    - B. Employers' Liability Under Statutes
        - 1. Choice of Law
        - 2. Persons and Employments Covered
        - 3. Injuries and Diseases Covered
        - 4. Benefits Provided
        - 5. Procedures for Obtaining Benefits
    - C. Federal Compensation Laws
        - 1. Longshore and Harbor Workers' Compensation Act
        - 2. Extensions of the LHWCA
        - 3. Federal Employers' Liability Act
        - 4. Migrant and Seasonal Agricultural Worker Protection Act
        - 5. The Federal Employees' Compensation Act

- ▶ **Environmental Liability Loss Exposures**
    - A. Environmental Liability Causes of Loss
        - 1. Tort
        - 2. Contract
        - 3. Statute

- ▶ **Professional Liability Loss Exposures**
    - A. Professional Liability Causes of Loss
        - 1. Tort
        - 2. Contract
        - 3. Statute
    - B. Physicians' Professional Liability Loss Exposures
    - C. Accountants' Professional Liability Loss Exposures
    - D. Insurance Agents' and Brokers' Professional Liability Loss Exposures
    - E. Architects' and Engineers' Professional Liability Loss Exposures

- ▶ **Summary**

When you take the randomized full practice exams in the SMART Online Practice Exams product, you are using the same software you will use when you take the actual exam. Take advantage of your time and learn the features of the software now.

▶▶

For each assignment, you should define or describe each of the Key Words and Phrases and answer each of the Review and Application Questions.

Educational Objective 1

Describe the liability loss exposures arising out of workers' compensation.

Key Words and Phrases

Statutory employee (p. 6.7)

Positional risk doctrine (p. 6.8)

Review Questions

1-1. Identify the specific duties an employer must exercise regarding employee safety that have been derived from the common-law reasonable duty of care. (p. 6.4)

1-2. Identify the available defenses to employers in cases where the employer is not barred from relying on common-law defenses. (p. 6.4)

1-3. Identify the principles of the workers' compensation system.
      (pp. 6.5–6.6)

1-4. Describe the common features of state workers' compensation
      laws. (pp. 6.6–6.11)

1-5. Explain who is usually responsible for workers' compensation
      insurance covering leased employees. (pp. 6.7–6.8)

1-6. With regard to occupational injuries, what must an employee
      seeking workers' compensation benefits typically show? (p. 6.8)

1-7. With regard to occupational diseases, what must an employee
      seeking workers' compensation benefits typically show? (p. 6.8)

1-8. Identify the types of benefits provided under workers' compensation statutes. (p. 6.9)

1-9. Describe the disability classifications used in workers' compensation statutes. (p. 6.10)

1-10. Identify some of the federal compensation programs that provide coverage for individuals not eligible for state workers' compensation benefits. (p. 6.11)

1-11. Identify some of the federal statutes that extend the benefits of the Longshoremen and Harbor Workers' Compensation Act (LHWCA) to additional classes of employees. (p. 6.13)

Application Question

1-12. Office Complex hires Window Company to replace old
defective windows in all the office buildings located in
one of its office parks. What documentation should Office
Complex obtain from Window Company regarding its workers'
compensation coverage before the work begins?

Educational Objective 2

Describe the liability loss exposures arising out of environmental pollution.

Review Questions

2-1.   Identify the legal bases under which an organization can incur
environmental liability. (p. 6.14)

2-2.   Identify the most frequent causes of environmental losses.
(p. 6.14)

2-3. Identify some of the possible consequences set forth in environmental statute provisions for noncompliance regarding reactive, corrosive, toxic, or flammable materials. (p. 6.16)

2-4. Identify the major federal environmental laws. (p. 6.17)

2-5. Describe the role of potentially responsible parties (PRPs) in a Superfund site. (p. 6.19)

2-6. Identify entities that may be potentially responsible parties (PRPs). (p. 6.20)

2-7. Identify the defenses to liability under the Comprehensive Environmental Response, Compensation, and Liability Act (CERCLA). (p. 6.21)

Application Question

2-8. Explain the focus of each of the following federal environmental laws:

   a. Clean Air Act (p. 6.18)

   b. Resource Conservation and Recovery Act (RCRA) (p. 6.18)

   c. Motor Carrier Act (p. 6.19)

   d. Comprehensive Environmental Response, Compensation, and Liability Act (CERCLA) (p. 6.19)

Educational Objective 3

Describe the liability loss exposures arising out of professional activities, including physicians, accountants, insurance agents and brokers, and architects and engineers.

Review Questions

3-1.   Identify the occupations traditionally considered to be professions. (p. 6.22)

3-2.   Identify professional liability loss exposures for the following:

   a. Physicians (p. 6.25)

   b. Accountants (p. 6.26)

   c. Insurance agents and brokers (p. 6.27)

   d. Architects and engineers (p. 6.28)

3-3. Identify the type of information that a physician must dis-
      close in obtaining informed consent before treating a patient.
      (p. 6.25)

Application Question

3-4. Identify if a physicians' professional liability loss exposure exists
      in each of the following situations:

   a. A physician fails to diagnose and consequently treat a
      patient's illness.

   b. A patient slips on a damp floor while walking from the
      reception area to an examination room.

   c. A physician correctly diagnoses a patient with cancer and
      chooses to treat the patient rather than refer the patient to a
      cancer specialist.

Answers to Assignment 6 Questions

NOTE: These answers are provided to give students a basic understanding of acceptable types of responses. They often are not the only valid answers and are not intended to provide an exhaustive response to the questions.

Educational Objective 1

1-1.   The specific duties an employer must exercise regarding employee safety are as follows:
- Providing a safe place to work
- Providing competent fellow employees
- Providing safe tools and equipment
- Warning employees of inherent dangers
- Making and enforcing rules for the safety of all employees

1-2.   In cases where the employer is not barred from relying on common-law defenses, the employer may have the following available defenses:
- Contributory negligence
- Comparative negligence
- Negligence of a fellow employee
- Statute of limitations

1-3.   The principles of the workers' compensation system are as follows:
- Provide sure, prompt, and reasonable income and medical benefits to work-accident victims or income benefits to their dependents, regardless of fault
- Provide a single remedy and reduce court delays, costs, and workloads arising out of personal injury litigation
- Relieve public and private charities of financially draining incidents associated with uncompensated industrial accidents
- Eliminate payments of fees to lawyers and witnesses as well as time-consuming trials and appeals
- Encourage maximum employer interest in safety and rehabilitation through appropriate experience rating mechanisms
- Promote frank study of causes of accidents, thereby reducing the number of preventable accidents and consequent human suffering

1-4.   The common features of state workers' compensation laws are as follows:
- Choice of law—the laws of different states can apply in an employment-related injury depending on the place of injury, the place of hire, the place of employment, the location of the employer, the residence of the employee, and any state whose workers' compensation laws are adopted by contract.
- Persons and employments covered—statutes cover most public and private employments. Generally, an employer's obligation does not extend to independent contractors.
- Injuries and diseases covered—statutes provide benefits for occupational injury and some occupational diseases.

- Benefits provided—statutes provide medical benefits, disability benefits, rehabilitation services, and death benefits.
- Procedures for obtaining benefits—to obtain benefits, the injured employee is required to notify the employer within a certain time period. The employee or employee's survivor is required to file a claim for compensation within a designated time.

1-5. The professional employer organization (PEO) is usually responsible for workers' compensation insurance covering leased employees. Generally, a separate workers' compensation policy is purchased in the names of the PEO and the client organization, although the requirements imposed by law vary by state.

1-6. With regard to occupational injuries, an employee seeking workers' compensation benefits must typically show the following:
- He or she suffered an injury caused by an accident
- The injury arose out of employment
- The injury occurred in the course of employment

1-7. With regard to occupational diseases, an employee seeking workers' compensation benefits must typically show the following:
- The disease is covered by the statute as one that normally results from the nature of the employment
- The exposure to the disease arose from employment

1-8. The types of benefits provided under workers' compensation statutes are as follows:
- Medical benefits
- Disability benefits
- Rehabilitation services
- Death benefits

1-9. The disability classifications used in workers' compensation statutes are as follows:
- Temporary total disability—the injured worker is expected to recover fully, but until recovery is achieved, the injured worker is unable to work at all.
- Permanent total disability—the injured worker will never be able to return to gainful employment.
- Temporary partial disability—the injured worker can return to work in some capacity and eventually will be able to perform the job held before the occurrence of the injury or disease.
- Permanent partial disability—the injured worker is permanently limited in some respect.

1-10. Federal compensation programs that provide coverage for individuals not eligible for state workers' compensation benefits include the following:
- Longshore and Harbor Workers' Compensation Act (LHWCA)
- Extensions of the LHWCA
- Federal Employers' Liability Act
- Migrant and Seasonal Agricultural Worker Protection Act
- Federal Employees' Compensation Act

1-11.   Federal statutes that extend the benefits of the Longshoremen and Harbor Workers' Compensation Act (LHWCA) to additional classes of employees include the following:

- Defense Base Act
- Outer Continental Shelf Lands Act
- Nonappropriated Fund Instrumentalities Act

1-12.   Office Complex should require Window Company to provide it with a certificate of insurance that shows valid workers' compensation insurance in effect. Also, Office Complex should have its own workers' compensation insurance in case the certificate of insurance later proves to be ineffective.

Educational Objective 2

2-1.   The legal bases under which an organization can incur environmental liability are tort, contract, or statute.

2-2.   The most frequent causes of environmental losses are the following:

- Actual or alleged release of pollutants
- Violation of a law designed to protect human health and the environment from pollutants
- Enforcement of environmental protection laws that require remediation expense payment

2-3.   Possible consequences for noncompliance set forth by environmental statutes regarding reactive, corrosive, toxic, or flammable materials include injunctions, fines, and other penalties, such as revocation of permits. The statutes also contain provisions for the criminal prosecution of individuals, including corporate officers.

2-4.   The major federal environmental laws are as follows:

- The National Environmental Policy Act (1969)
- Clean Air Act (1969)
- Clean Water Act (1970)
- Toxic Substance Control Act (1979)
- Resource Conservation and Recovery Act (RCRA) (1979)
- Motor Carrier Act (1980)
- Comprehensive Environmental Response, Compensation, and Liability Act (CERCLA) (1980)
- Oil Pollution Act (1990)

2-5.   Potentially responsible parties (PRPs) are persons or entities that are potentially legally responsible for the costs of remediating a Superfund site.

2-6.   Entities that may be potentially responsible parties (PRPs) include the following:

- Current owners and operators of a site
- Prior owners and operators who may or may not have been involved with the site during the disposal of hazardous material
- Generators of the waste material disposed of at the site
- Transporters who hauled waste to the site
- Anyone who arranged for disposal at the site

2-7.   The defenses to liability under CERCLA are as follows:
- Acts of God
- Acts of war
- Acts of an unrelated third party

2-8.   a.   Clean Air Act—regulates emissions from mobile and stationary sources of air pollution

    b.   Resource Conservation and Recovery Act (RCRA)—regulates hazardous waste management and imposes strict requirements on generators and transporters of hazardous waste and on hazardous waste treatment, storage, and disposal

    c.   Motor Carrier Act— seeks to protect the environment from releases of harmful materials during transport by motor carriers in interstate or intrastate commerce

    d.   Comprehensive Environmental Response, Compensation, and Liability Act—facilitates the cleanup of abandoned or uncontrolled sites containing hazardous substances

Educational Objective 3

3-1.   Occupations traditionally considered to be professions include law, medicine, education, and the clergy.

3-2.   Professional liability loss exposures for the professions cited are as follows:

    a.   Physicians—surgery, diagnosis, diagnostic tests, and consent

    b.   Accountants—tax services, audit services, accounting services, and securities laws

    c.   Insurance agents and brokers—failure to obtain insurance or the correct coverage requested by their client

    d.   Architects and engineers—practicing beyond the scope of the license, conflict of interest, negligently prepared plans or designs, negligently performed site surveys, negligent materials or equipment selection, negligent construction supervision, and increased construction costs

3-3.   A physician must disclose the following information before treating a patient:
- The nature of the condition or problem
- The nature or purpose of the proposed procedure or treatment
- The risks associated with the proposed procedure or treatment
- The anticipated benefits (results) of the proposed procedure on treatment
- Alternative procedures or treatments and the risks associated with them

3-4.   a.   This is a physicians' liability loss exposure because it arises out of the physician's duties as a physician.

    b.   This is not a physicians' liability loss exposure because it does not arise out of the physician's duty as a physician.

    c.   This is a physicians' liability loss exposure because it arises out of the physician's duty as a physician.

▶▶

Direct Your Learning

Assessing Management Liability Loss Exposures

Educational Objectives

After learning the content of this assignment, you should be able to:

1. Describe the liability loss exposures of a corporation arising out of directors' and officers' responsibilities.

2. Describe the liability loss exposures of an organization arising out of its employment practices.

3. Describe the liability loss exposures of an organization arising out of its employee benefit plans.

4. Define or describe each of the Key Words and Phrases for this assignment.

Study Materials

Required Reading:
▶ Risk Assessment
  • Chapter 7

Study Aids:
▶ SMART Online Practice Exams
▶ SMART Study Aids
  • Review Notes and Flash Cards— Assignment 7

Outline

▶ **Directors' and Officers' Liability Loss Exposures**

A. The Corporation and the Role of Directors and Officers

B. Types of Lawsuits Made Against Directors and Officers

C. Directors' and Officers' Major Responsibilities and Duties

    1. Duty of Care

    2. Duty of Loyalty

    3. Duty of Disclosure

    4. Duty of Obedience

D. Directors' and Officers' Responsibilities Under the Securities Laws

    1. Securities Act of 1933

    2. Securities Exchange Act of 1934

    3. Private Securities Litigation Reform Act of 1995

    4. Sarbanes-Oxley Act of 2002

E. Indemnification of Directors and Officers

▶ **Employment Practices Liability Loss Exposures**

A. Discrimination Lawsuits

    1. Overt Discrimination, Disparate Treatment, and Disparate Impact

    2. Equal Employment Opportunity Commission

B. Wrongful Termination Lawsuits

C. Sexual Harassment Lawsuits

D. Retaliation Lawsuits

E. Other Types of EPL Lawsuits

▶ **Fiduciary Liability Loss Exposures From Employee Benefit Plans**

A. Employee Retirement Income Security Act of 1974 (ERISA)

B. Duties and Liabilities of Employee Benefit Plan Fiduciaries

C. Health Insurance Portability and Accountability Act (HIPAA)

▶ **Summary**

 Set aside a specific, realistic amount of time to study every day.

For each assignment, you should define or describe each of the Key Words and Phrases and answer each of the Review and Application Questions.

Educational Objective 1
Describe the liability loss exposures of a corporation arising out of directors' and officers' responsibilities.

Key Words and Phrases
Derivative lawsuit (p. 7.5)

Class action, or class action lawsuit (p. 7.7)

Fiduciary duty (p. 7.8)

Business judgment rule (p. 7.8)

Swing trading (p. 7.14)

Review Questions
1-1. Distinguish between a public corporation and a private corporation. (p. 7.4)

1-2.   Explain how a corporation's directors are elected. (p. 7.4)

1-3.   Other than corporations, identify entities that have management liability loss exposures. (p. 7.4)

1-4.   Identify the typical allegations made against directors and officers in a securities class action complaint. (p. 7.7)

1-5.   List the major responsibilities of corporate directors. (pp. 7.7–7.8)

1-6.   What is the Model Business Corporation Act's definition of "duty of care"? (p. 7.8)

1-7. Identify the provisions that the business judgment rule grants regarding liability of directors and officers. (pp. 7.8–7.9)

1-8. Give examples of persons to whom directors and officers are obliged to disclose information under their duty of disclosure. (p. 7.10)

1-9. Describe the following securities laws:

a. Securities Act of 1933 (pp. 7.11–7.13)

b. Securities Exchange Act of 1934 (pp. 7.13–7.14)

c. Private Securities Litigation Reform Act of 1995 (p. 7.15)

    d. Sarbanes-Oxley Act of 2002 (pp. 7.15–7.17)

1-10. Identify why it is important for a corporation to provide indemnification to its directors and officers. (p. 7.17)

1-11. Describe the business corporation legislation regarding indemnification provided by the following: (p. 7.18)

    a. Model Business Corporation Act

    b. Delaware law

1-12. Identify how an organization might adopt guidelines for reimbursement. (p. 7.18)

Application Question

1-13. Categorize the following lawsuits as either a derivative or non-derivative lawsuit. (p. 7.5)

  a. Fast Food Restaurant Chain's marketing ploy, a sweepstakes, is found to be tainted by fraud. Consequently, thousands of customers bring suit in their own names against the directors and officers.

  b. Fast Food Restaurant Chain's marketing ploy, a sweepstakes, is found to be tainted by fraud. Consequentially, shareholders bring suit against the directors and officers in the name of the corporation.

Educational Objective 2
Describe the liability loss exposures of an organization arising out of its employment practices.

Key Words and Phrases

Overt discrimination (p. 7.22)

Disparate treatment (p. 7.22)

Disparate impact (p. 7.23)

Wrongful termination lawsuits (p. 7.24)

At-will employment (p. 7.24)

Hostile work environment (p. 7.25)

Review Questions

2-1. Describe three factors that have contributed to a rapid expansion in employment practices liability (EPL) loss exposures. (p. 7.19)

2-2. Identify the major types of EPL lawsuits. (p. 7.20)

2-3. Explain the role of the Equal Employment Opportunity Commission (EEOC) in situations involving discrimination. (p. 7.23)

2-4.   What must be proved in a wrongful termination lawsuit? (p. 7.24)

2-5.   Explain how an at-will employment relationship can be altered. (p. 7.24)

2-6.   According to the EEOC's Web site, identify circumstances in which sexual harassment can occur. (p. 7.25)

2-7.   Identify the facts that must be shown to prove a claim of hostile work environment. (p. 7.25)

Application Question

2-8.   For each of the following situations, categorize it as either overt discrimination, disparate treatment, or disparate impact:

   a. City Police Force creates a pay scale that favors younger police officers.

   b. Real Estate Agency decides that non-Caucasian sales representatives do not present the image it prefers, and it chooses not to hire non-Caucasians.

   c. General Contractor requires manual laborers have a high school diploma, thereby limiting the number of qualified minority workers.

Educational Objective 3

Describe the liability loss exposures of an organization arising out of its employee benefit plans.

Review Questions

3-1.   Describe the duties of an employee benefit plan fiduciary.
(p. 7.28)

3-2.   Describe the possible consequences of a breach of duty that
results in loss to a benefit plan. (pp. 7.28–7.29)

3-3.   Explain what the Health and Insurance Portability and
Accountability Act of 1996 (HIPAA) is designed to do. (p.
7.29)

Application Question

3-4.   Office Products Company shares employee health data with
a potential merger candidate. Determine the amount of the
penalty under HIPAA if 100 employees' records are involved.

Answers to Assignment 7 Questions

NOTE: These answers are provided to give students a basic understanding of acceptable types of responses. They often are not the only valid answers and are not intended to provide an exhaustive response to the questions.

Educational Objective 1

1-1. A public corporation is a corporation whose shares are traded to and among the public on the open market. A private corporation is a corporation whose shares are not traded on the open market.

1-2. A corporation's directors are elected by its shareholders in accordance with the corporation's bylaws.

1-3. Other than corporations, entities that have management liability loss exposures include the following:
- Public bodies
- Not-for-profit organizations
- Trusts
- Limited liability companies
- Limited partnerships

1-4. Allegations brought against directors and officers in a securities class action complaint typically include the following:
- The company's public statements contained material misrepresentations or omissions.
- The alleged misrepresentations or omissions artificially inflated the company's share price.
- While the share price was artificially inflated, insiders profitably sold their personal holdings in the company's shares.
- After the insider sales were completed, the company's share price dropped sharply when the company divulged information inconsistent with the earlier statements that had inflated the share price.

1-5. The major responsibilities of corporate directors are as follows:
- To establish the basic objectives and broad policies of the corporation
- To elect or appoint corporate officers, advise them, approve their actions, and audit their performance
- To safeguard and approve changes in the corporation's assets
- To approve important financial matters and see that proper annual and interim reports are given to shareholders
- To delegate special powers to others to sign contracts, open bank accounts, sign checks, issue shares, make loans, and conduct activities that may require board approval
- To maintain, revise, and enforce the corporate charter and bylaws
- To perpetuate a competent board through regular elections and the filling of interim vacancies with qualified persons
- To act as a fiduciary in their relationship to the corporation and its shareholders

1-6. The Model Business Corporation Act's definition of "duty of care" is the care that a person in a like position would reasonably believe appropriate under similar circumstances.

1-7. The business judgment rule grants immunity from liability to directors and officers if they made an informed decision and they acted in good faith.

1-8. Under the duty of disclosure, directors and officers are obliged to share facts that are material to the following:

- Directors
- Various regulatory bodies
- Creditors or potential creditors
- Shareholders, bondholders, and potential investors in the securities of the corporation

1-9. Directors and officers are affected by the following securities laws:

a. Securities Act of 1933—governs the issuing of securities and enables purchasers of registered securities to recover damages from the corporation's directors if the registration statement to the Security Exchange Commission contains a material omission or misrepresentation. The legal action must be filed within three years of the purchase and within one year of discovering the misstatement or omission.

b. Securities Exchange Act of 1934—governs transactions that occur after securities have been issued and enables purchasers of registered securities to recover damages from the corporation's directors if financial reports filed with the Securities and Exchange Commission contain a material omission or misrepresentation. The legal action must be filed within three years of the security's purchase or within one year of discovering the misstatement or omission.

c. Private Securities Litigation Reform Act of 1995—addresses abuses in securities litigation and was designed to prevent frivolous lawsuits. It provides protection from liability if a director makes a forward-looking statement about the corporation's future financial performance without acknowledging that factors could cause actual results to differ materially. Protection is not provided in cases in which a director's forward-looking statements are known to be false.

d. Sarbanes-Oxley Act of 2002—aimed at protecting investors. It requires the chief executive officer (CEO) and chief financial officer (CFO) to certify the accuracy of a corporation's quarterly and annual financial reports, and liability arises if the CEO and CFO knowingly and intentionally fail to comply. The act prohibits directors from buying or selling shares acquired in connection with their employment during pension plan blackouts. The corporation, or shareholders if the corporation fails to take action, may sue directors for profits earned in trading shares during a blackout period.

1-10. It is important for a corporation to provide indemnification to directors and officers because indemnification provides compensation for the losses the directors and officers sustain because of lawsuits based on their participation as board members. This provision of indemnification helps the organization obtain the services of qualified people.

1-11. Business corporation legislation regarding indemnification includes the following:

a. Model Business Corporation Act—forbids indemnification when directors only partially vindicate themselves. In a derivative lawsuit, expense indemnification is permitted even when the director is liable.

b. Delaware law—encourages indemnification even when directors only partially vindicate themselves. In a derivative lawsuit, court approval is required for indemnification when a director is liable.

1-12. An organization might adopt guidelines for reimbursement through incorporation into the bylaws, a corporate resolution, or other written agreements, such as an employment contract.

1-13. The lawsuits cited can be categorized as follows:

a. Customer suit—because the lawsuit against the directors and officers is being brought by individuals, and not in the name of the corporation, this is a nonderivative lawsuit.

b. Shareholder suit—because the lawsuit against the directors and officers is being brought in the name of the corporation, this is a derivative lawsuit.

Educational Objective 2

2-1. Three factors that have contributed to a rapid expansion in employment practices liability (EPL) loss exposures are as follows:

(1) Changes in the employee-employer relationship

(2) Changes in the makeup of the workforce

(3) Changes in laws

2-2. The major types of EPL lawsuits are as follows:

- Discrimination lawsuits
- Wrongful termination lawsuits
- Sexual harassment lawsuits
- Retaliation lawsuits

2-3. The role of the Equal Employment Opportunity Commission (EEOC) in situations involving discrimination is to define acts of employment discrimination, attempt to mitigate the effects of employment discrimination by education and conciliation, and enforce employment standards by filing discrimination suits based on pattern or practice.

2-4. To prove a wrongful termination lawsuit, the employee (plaintiff) must prove that termination was without cause and violated an express or implied contract of employment, that the termination was the result of discrimination, or that the termination was against public policy.

2-5. An at-will employment relationship can be altered by creating an implied contract with the employee. Such a contract is formed if the employer has made oral or written representations to the employee regarding job security or disciplinary procedures.

2-6. The EEOC's Web site identifies the following circumstances that may lead to a sexual harassment claim:

- Victim or harasser may be a man or woman. The victim does not have to be of the opposite sex.
- Harasser's conduct must be unwelcome.
- Harasser can be the victim's supervisor, agent of the employer, supervisor in another area, co-worker, or a nonemployee.
- Victim can be anyone affected by the offensive conduct.
- Unlawful sexual harassment may occur without economic injury or discharge of the victim.

2-7. To prove a claim of hostile work environment, an employee must generally show the following:

- He or she is a member of a protected class.
- He or she was subjected to unwelcome harassment based on the protected characteristic.
- The harassment affected a term or condition of employment.
- The employer knew or should have known about the harassment and failed to take prompt remedial action.

2-8. The situations are characterized as follows:

a. City Police Force's pay scale—disparate impact

b. Real Estate Agency's hiring—overt discrimination

c. General Contractor's hiring—disparate treatment

Educational Objective 3

3-1. The duties of an employee benefit plan fiduciary are as follows:

- Care—duties must be carried out with care, skill, prudence, and diligence of a prudent person familiar with such matters.
- Loyalty—actions must be solely in the best interests of the plan, participants, and beneficiaries.
- Diversification—the plan's investments must be sufficiently diversified to minimize the risk of large losses.
- Obedience—actions must be according to plan documents and applicable law.

3-2. The possible consequences of a breach of duty that results in loss to a benefit plan are as follows:

- Fiduciary is personally liable to the plan for the full amount of the loss.
- Fiduciary might be subject to a fine.
- Fiduciary might be subject to an action for damages brought by a plan participant.
- Fiduciary might be liable for a breach of duty by another fiduciary if the first fiduciary knowingly participates in the breach, conceals it, or makes no attempt to correct it.
- Employer might be held vicariously liable for breaches of fiduciary duty and may be able to recover its share of damages from the employee or agent.

3-3. The Health and Insurance Portability and Accountability Act of 1996 (HIPAA) is designed to do the following:

- Set standards for health insurance "portability" by providing a credit against preexisting condition exclusion periods for prior health coverage
- Limit exclusions for preexisting medical conditions
- Prohibit discrimination in enrollment and in premiums charged to employees and their dependents based on health-related factors
- Improve disclosure about group health plans
- Protect employee medical information

3-4. Office Products Company could be fined $10,000 (100 employees × $100). Additionally, the persons who disclosed the information may be subject to fines and imprisonment.

▶▶

Direct Your Learning

Understanding Corporate Governance

Educational Objectives

After learning the content of this assignment, you should be able to:

1. Explain how separation of ownership and control leads to agency costs.

2. Describe the three categories of agency costs.

3. Describe four mechanisms to align manager and shareholder interests.

4. Describe the relationship between value maximization and social responsibility.

5. Explain how boards of directors are composed to meet corporate governance expectations.

6. Describe the five key issues in corporate governance.

7. Describe the responsibility of corporate governance as it relates to risk management.

8. Define or describe each of the Key Words and Phrases for this assignment.

Study Materials

Required Reading:
▶ Risk Assessment
  • Chapter 8

Study Aids:
▶ SMART Online Practice Exams
▶ SMART Study Aids
  • Review Notes and Flash Cards— Assignment 8

Outline

▶ **Role of Corporate Governance**

    A. Separation of Ownership and Control

    B. Value Maximization and Social Responsibility

▶ **Board Composition and Directors' Legal Obligations**

    A. Board Composition

    B. Directors' Legal Obligations

▶ **Key Issues in Corporate Governance**

    A. Pressures from Shareholder Expectations and Behavior

    B. Executive Incentives and Compensation

    C. Accountability of Directors

    D. Corporate Financial Reporting

    E. Importance of Integrity

▶ **Corporate Governance and Risk Management**

▶ **Summary**

 Plan to take one week to complete each assignment in your course.

For each assignment, you should define or describe each of the Key Words and Phrases and answer each of the Review and Application Questions.

Educational Objective 1

Explain how separation of ownership and control leads to agency costs.

Key Word or Phrase

Corporate governance (p. 8.3)

Review Questions

1-1. Contrast organizational goals for not-for-profit and for-profit organizations. (p. 8.4)

1-2. How does the limited liability of shareholders facilitate the separation of ownership and control? (p. 8.4)

1-3. Identify economic benefits to a corporation and to consumers provided by separation of ownership and control. (p. 8.5)

Application Question

1-4. Atwell Corporation's board of directors is considering two merger candidates. The first candidate will enhance the prestige of the corporation among its industry peers. The second candidate will allow the corporation to have easy access to international markets. Which merger candidate would Atwell's shareholders most likely want the board of directors to choose and why? (p. 8.4)

Educational Objective 2

Describe the three categories of agency costs.

Key Word or Phrase

Agency costs (p. 8.5)

Review Questions

2-1. Describe monitoring costs and identify the person in an organization who bears the majority of these costs. (p. 8.5)

2-2. Describe bonding costs and identify the person in an organization who bears the majority of these costs. (p. 8.5)

2-3. Describe incentive alignment costs and identify the person in an organization who bears the majority of these costs. (p. 8.5)

2-4. Explain how a manager's averse attitude to risk can result in additional agency costs. (p. 8.6)

Application Question

2-5. Atwell Corporation's executives have been promised significant bonuses if a merger is completed this year. What costs, if any, will Atwell incur to ensure that the merger is in the best interests of its shareholders? (p. 8.5)

Educational Objective 3

Describe four mechanisms to align manager and shareholder interests.

Review Questions

3-1.   Describe the four main mechanisms used to align manager and shareholder interests. (p. 8.6)

3-2.   How did some states respond to the wave of hostile takeovers in the 1980s? (p. 8.7)

3-3.   Identify one strategy that corporations have instituted to deter a hostile takeover. (p. 8.8)

Application Question

3-4. Atwell's merger was completed; however, the value of Atwell's shares fell because the marketplace perceived the merged organization to be of lesser value. Which, if any, of the mechanisms relied on to align manager and stockholder interests may come into play now?

Educational Objective 4

Describe the relationship between value maximization and social responsibility.

Review Questions

4-1. Identify the reasons why maximizing a corporation's economic value (value maximization) appropriately serves the overall interests of society. (p. 8.8)

4-2. Describe how an organization might decrease the chance of conflict between maximizing corporate economic value and societal goals. (pp. 8.8–8.9)

4-3. Describe how the legal system might mitigate conflicts between corporate value maximization goals and the interests of stakeholders. (p. 8.9)

Application Question

4-4. Explain how the legal system can reallocate the costs to society of those of Atwell's corporate decisions that are at odds with the well-being of society. (p. 8.9)

Educational Objective 5

Explain how boards of directors are composed to meet corporate governance expectations.

Key Words and Phrases

Audit committee (p. 8.11)

Compensation committee (p. 8.11)

Nominations/corporate governance committee (p. 8.11)

Review Questions

5-1. Explain how separation of oversight and control for corporate boards of directors is being accomplished. (p. 8.9)

5-2. Describe the functions of the three most important corporate board committees. (p. 8.11)

5-3. Describe the two sources of legal liability for corporate directors. (p. 8.11)

Application Question

5-4. Atwell Corporation has been illegally dumping toxic waste into a local river. The Environmental Protection Agency (EPA) recently notified Atwell that it must cease and desist operations until it corrects the problem. Why should Atwell's directors and officers be concerned with this pollution? (p. 8.12)

Educational Objective 6

Describe the five key issues in corporate governance.

Review Questions

6-1. Identify the five corporate governance issues that affect a corporation's long-term economic value creation. (p. 8.13)

6-2. Identify incentives and compensation that may be provided to executives of a corporation. (p. 8.14)

6-3. Describe the possible consequences if integrity is lacking in an organization. (p. 8.18)

Application Question

6-4. Atwell's shareholders are concerned that its present incentive compensation program encourages management to make short-term decisions that are not necessarily good decisions in the long term. How might Atwell's incentive compensation program be changed to promote long-term economic value creation?

Educational Objective 7

Describe the responsibility of corporate governance as it relates to risk management.

Review Questions

7-1. Identify events that have led corporate boards to become increasingly concerned with risk management issues. (p. 8.19)

7-2. In the context of corporate governance, identify the risk management responsibilities of directors and officers. (p. 8.19)

7-3. Identify the overall goal of corporate governance regarding risk control. (p. 8.19)

Application Question

7-4. Atwell's failure to abide by environmental regulations can be seen as a breakdown in the risk management process. What type of pressure may have led Atwell to violate these regulations? (p. 8.20)

Answers to Assignment 8 Questions

NOTE: These answers are provided to give students a basic understanding of acceptable types of responses. They often are not the only valid answers and are not intended to provide an exhaustive response to the questions.

Educational Objective 1

1-1.   Not-for-profit corporations' organizational goal is to maximize the value of goods or services provided to their various constituencies. For-profit corporations' organizational goal is to maximize the value of shareholders' shares, which in turn generally requires maximization of the corporation's total economic value.

1-2.   Limited liability of shareholders facilitates separation of ownership and control because if shareholders had their personal wealth at risk from corporate decisions, many more of them would seek to play an active role in corporate decision making.

1-3.   Economic benefits of separation of ownership and control to a corporation and to consumers include reduced cost of capital; increased productive investment; and better, more affordable, products.

1-4.   Shareholders generally want managers to make decisions that maximize the value of their shares. In this case, while corporate prestige can add value to shareholders, access to international markets would probably maximize the value of shares of the corporation. Therefore, shareholders would most likely prefer the second candidate.

Educational Objective 2

2-1.   Monitoring costs are the first category of agency costs that are incurred monitoring the corporate decision makers. The majority of monitoring costs are borne by the shareholders.

2-2.   Bonding costs are the second category of agency costs that are incurred to show that managers are serving (or will serve) the shareholders' interests. The majority of bonding costs are incurred by the managers.

2-3.   Incentive alignment costs are the third category of agency costs and are the reduction in value of an organization because the incentives of corporate decision makers are not perfectly aligned with shareholders' interests. The majority of incentive alignment costs are incurred by the shareholders.

2-4.   Risk-averse managers might avoid projects that are perceived as too risky even though these projects could increase the corporation's economic value. Managers might also devote more corporate resources to risk reduction or risk transfer than would be necessary to maximize the value of the corporation's shares.

2-5.   Of the three categories of agency costs—monitoring costs, bonding costs, and incentive alignment costs—bonding costs are the one borne by the corporation. In this case, the bonding costs are the costs that Atwell needs to incur to ensure that any merger considered by the corporation's executives is in the best interests of the shareholders.

Educational Objective 3

3-1.   The four main mechanisms used to align manager and shareholder interests are as follows:

(1) Incentive compensation—mangers' compensation is linked to the corporation's economic performance.

(2) Legal liability—directors and officers can be held personally liable to shareholders for any harm from their decisions.

(3) Management reputation—managers who make decisions that do not increase the corporation's economic value can develop reputations for being poor managers.

(4) Takeover threats—managers who fail to make decisions to maximize the value of the corporation's stock often increase the probability that another corporation will acquire the corporation.

3-2.   In response to the wave of hostile takeovers in the 1980s, many states enacted anti-takeover statutes that made a hostile takeover more difficult.

3-3.   To deter hostile takeovers, some corporations have changed their corporate charters or introduced staggered terms for directors so that acquirers will have more difficulty taking control after a takeover.

3-4.   Of the four mechanisms used to align manager and shareholder interests—incentive compensation, legal liability, management reputation, and takeover threats—the most direct mechanism is legal liability. Shareholders often file class action suits against corporations that do not act in their best interests. Management reputation and takeover threats can still be useful mechanisms in this case; however, legal liability is the most direct mechanism.

Educational Objective 4

4-1.   Maximizing a corporation's economic value is considered an appropriate organizational goal because the pursuit of this goal promotes economic efficiency, innovation, and growth, leading to higher standards of living than would otherwise be possible.

4-2.   An organization might decrease the chance of conflict between maximizing corporate economic value and societal goals by weighing the effects of decisions on employees, customers, suppliers, and lenders in order to attract and retain these stakeholders. Actions that harm them are generally bad for business and therefore bad for shareholders.

4-3.   The legal system might mitigate conflicts between corporate value maximization goals and the interests of shareholders by providing incentives for corporate decision makers to consider the effects of their decisions on non-investor stakeholders when market forces do not promote such consideration.

4-4.   The legal system, through holding corporations legally liable for their actions or decisions that have a negative effect on stakeholders, helps internalize the cost of corporate decisions. In other words, it forces the corporation to account for all of the negative effects that their decisions may have on others.

Educational Objective 5

5-1. Separation of oversight and control for corporate boards of directors is being accomplished by the following:

- Requiring a majority of directors be outside directors
- Requiring regular meetings of outside directors without management present
- Requiring key committees to be composed of only outside directors

5-2. The three most important corporate board committees are as follows:

   (1) Audit committee—oversees the preparation and dissemination of the corporation's financial statements in conjunction with the corporation's external auditors

   (2) Compensation committee—determines the compensation arrangements for the CEO and other senior managers

   (3) Nominations/corporate governance committee—recommends nominees for election to the board by shareholders and often establishes governance guidelines

5-3. The two sources of legal liability for corporate directors are as follows:

   (1) Common law—imposes duty of care, duty of loyalty, duty of disclosure, and duty of obedience on directors.

   (2) Statutory law—federal and state statutes create the bases for liability.

5-4. Atwell's directors and officers should be concerned because personal liability for violations of environmental statutes and regulations represent a significant source of risk for many directors and officers. They can be held personally liable under the Comprehensive Environmental Response Compensation and Liability Act of 1980 if they had personal knowledge and control of the contamination.

Educational Objective 6

6-1. The five corporate governance issues that affect a corporation's long-term economic value creation are as follows:

   (1) Pressures from shareholder expectations and behavior

   (2) Executive incentives and compensation

   (3) Accountability of directors

   (4) Corporate financial reporting

   (5) Importance of integrity

6-2. Incentives and compensation provided to executives of a corporation may include the following:

- Stock option grants
- Restricted stock grants
- Performance-related bonuses
- Deferred compensation

6-3. A lack of integrity can undermine public confidence and produce more costly monitoring, more costly rules and regulation, greater penalties for misconduct, and lower corporation values.

6-4.   Atwell's incentive compensation program may make some changes to move away from granting stock options and restrict top managers' influence over their own compensation. However, no consensus has been reached regarding best practices in terms of executive compensation to resolve this problem.

Educational Objective 7

7-1.   Corporate boards have become increasingly concerned with risk management issues because of recent stock market performance, corporate scandals, the Sarbanes-Oxley Act, and related changes in securities exchange listing requirements.

7-2.   In the context of corporate governance, the risk management responsibilities of directors and officers are as follows:

- Meeting or exceeding all legal and regulatory requirements related to risk management
- Disclosing material information about the corporation's risk and changes in its risk in a timely manner, including any events or risks that create the possibility of large uninsured losses
- Balancing the benefits and costs of strategic risk management decisions to increase the long-run economic value of the organization

7-3.   The overall goal of corporate governance regarding risk control is to ensure that the corporation invests in and employs all risk control techniques for which the expected reduction in harm to all parties exceeds the costs of the risk control techniques.

7-4.   Competition may have caused Atwell to try to increase its short-run earnings by cutting the costs of properly handling the toxic waste. While it may have been successful in the short-run, it will probably hurt long-run economic value now that Atwell is facing compliance sanctions from the EPA.

Direct Your Learning

Assessing Personnel Loss Exposures

Educational Objectives

After learning the content of this assignment, you should be able to:

1. Identify the personnel exposed to loss.

2. Describe the causes of loss affecting personnel loss exposures.

3. Describe the workplace hazards affecting personnel loss exposures.

4. Describe the financial consequences of personnel losses.

5. Explain how the following methods help risk managers assess personnel loss exposures:

    a. Risk assessment questionnaires

    b. Loss histories

    c. Other records and documents

    d. Flowcharts and organizational charts

    e. Personal inspections

    f. Expertise within and beyond the organization

6. Explain how demographic trends may affect an organization's personnel loss exposures.

7. Define or describe each of the Key Words and Phrases for this assignment.

Study Materials

Required Reading:
▶ Risk Assessment
  • Chapter 9

Study Aids:
▶ SMART Online Practice Exams
▶ SMART Study Aids
  • Review Notes and Flash Cards— Assignment 9

Outline

▶ **Personnel Exposed to Loss**
   A. Individual Employees
   B. Owners, Officers, and Managers
   C. Groups of Employees

▶ **Causes of Loss**
   A. Death
   B. Disability
   C. Resignation, Layoffs, and Firing
   D. Retirement
   E. Kidnap and Ransom
   F. War and Terrorism

▶ **Workplace Hazards**
   A. Poor Work Conditions
   B. Poor Compensation Packages
   C. Sexual Harassment
   D. Workplace Violence

▶ **Financial Consequences of Personnel Losses**
   A. Temporary Versus Permanent Losses
      1. Temporary Loss of an Individual
      2. Permanent Loss of an Individual
      3. Temporary or Permanent Loss of a Group
   B. Unique Consequences by Cause of Loss

▶ **Methods of Assessing Personnel Loss Exposures**
   A. Risk Assessment Questionnaires
   B. Loss Histories
   C. Other Records and Documents
   D. Flowcharts and Organizational Charts
   E. Personal Inspections
   F. Expertise Within and Beyond the Organization

▶ **Trends Affecting Personnel Loss Exposures**

▶ **Summary**

Try to establish a study area away from any distractions, to be used only for studying.

For each assignment, you should define or describe each of the Key Words and Phrases and answer each of the Review and Application Questions.

Educational Objective 1
Identify the personnel exposed to loss.

Review Questions

1-1. Identify the types of personnel whose absence from an organization might result in a personnel loss and therefore require risk management attention. (p. 9.3)

1-2. Describe the categories of key personnel within an organization that comprise personnel loss exposures. (pp. 9.4–9.5)

1-3. What must a risk management professional for a private business consider to ensure survival regarding the health and managerial competence of owners, officers, and managers? (p. 9.5)

Educational Objective 2
Describe the causes of loss affecting personnel loss exposures.

Key Words and Phrases
Mortality rate (p. 9.7)

Temporary total disability (p. 9.8)

Permanent total disability (p. 9.8)

Temporary partial disability (p. 9.8)

Permanent partial disability (p. 9.8)

Review Questions
2-1.   Identify possible causes of personnel losses. (p. 9.6)

2-2. Describe the following types of disability and their effect on an organization's personnel loss exposure: (p. 9.8)

a. Temporary total disability

b. Permanent total disability

c. Temporary partial disability

d. Permanent partial disability

2-3. Explain how the consequences of a layoff of employees may not be considered a personnel loss exposure. (p. 9.10)

Educational Objective 3

Describe the workplace hazards affecting personnel loss exposures.

Review Questions

3-1. Identify four workplace hazards that can increase the frequency of personnel losses. (pp. 9.14–9.15)

3-2. Describe the types of benefits that are included in an employee compensation package and how these benefits affect personnel losses. (p. 9.16)

3-3. Describe the effect that the 1991 Civil Rights Act has had on personnel loss exposures. (p. 9.16)

Educational Objective 4

Describe the financial consequences of personnel losses.

Review Questions

4-1.   Identify four financial consequences of personnel losses. (p. 9.19)

4-2.   Describe what a risk management professional needs to determine in handling a temporary or permanent loss of an individual employee. (pp. 9.19–9.20)

4-3.   Identify the financial consequences common to all causes of personnel loss. (p. 9.21)

Educational Objective 5

Explain how the following methods help risk managers assess personnel loss exposures:

a. Risk assessment questionnaires

b. Loss histories

c. Other records and documents

d. Flowcharts and organizational charts

e. Personal inspections

f. Expertise within and beyond the organization

Review Questions

5-1. Describe the strength and weakness of using risk assessment questionnaires in identifying personnel loss exposures. (p. 9.23)

5-2. Identify the types of information provided to the risk management professional by reviewing an organization's loss history. (p. 9.24)

5-3. Identify two insurance industry sources of information that are useful to a risk management professional in assessing an organization's potential personnel losses resulting from death or disability. (p. 9.24)

Educational Objective 6

Explain how demographic trends may affect an organization's personnel loss exposures.

Review Questions

6-1. Identify the types of demographic trends that might help risk management professionals forecast personnel losses. (p. 9.26)

6-2. Describe how the increasing age of the population may affect organizations. (p. 9.26)

6-3. Describe the effect of trends such as education and population migration on an organization's personnel loss exposures. (p. 9.27)

Application Questions

6-4.   Glass Art, Inc., is a small publicly traded corporation with ten
       employees. Glass Art produces extremely high-grade, hand-
       made, decorative glass items. These items are produced by two
       glass blowers, Martin Boyer and Tony Corley. Glass blowing
       involves melting glass rods using a furnace. One of these glass
       blowers, Martin, is responsible for creating many of Glass Art's
       distinctive designs. Martin is also responsible for the training of
       the four apprentice glass blowers.

   a. What questions should Glass Art, Inc., ask itself in
      determining the personnel exposed to loss?

   b. What are the causes of loss that are related to Glass Art's
      personnel exposures that may affect multiple employees?

   c. What can Glass Art do to minimize the likelihood that
      Martin and Tony will leave to go work for a competitor?

6-5. Bob and Tom Brown own 90 percent of the stock in Brown's Bakery, located in a small New England town where the main attraction is the local college. Bill Edwards, a longtime employee, owns the remaining stock. The Browns have built up the business to the point where they employ twenty people. Most of the bakery's employees are college students who have flexible-enough schedules to work the early morning hours before classes start. The bakery's main customers are the college students, workers at the machine shop down the street, and residents of the popular retirement community across the street. Bob is president of the company and devotes much of his time to sales. Tom is vice president and focuses on financial matters. Bill Edwards runs the bakery operations. Bill has recently returned to work after three months of recovery from surgery to correct a back injury sustained at work and is contemplating retirement. During Bill's recovery, the bakery's production dropped 20 percent. The bakery's owners have realized that with the growth of the company, they have paid too little attention to an important matter—personnel loss exposures—and have therefore hired Sheila Jones, a risk management consultant.

a. How can Sheila determine the financial consequences of Bill's retirement?

b. What methods of assessing personnel risks might Sheila use in determining the financial consequences of Bill's retirement?

c. What trends may affect the bakery's personnel loss exposures?

Answers to Assignment 9 Questions

NOTE: These answers are provided to give students a basic understanding of acceptable types of responses. They often are not the only valid answers and are not intended to provide an exhaustive response to the questions.

Educational Objective 1

1-1. The types of personnel whose absence from an organization might result in a personnel loss are key employees; that is, employees who possess a special skill or knowledge and are therefore difficult to replace and employees who perform essential functions.

1-2. The categories of key personnel within an organization that comprise personnel loss exposures are as follows:

- Individual employees—includes employees with unique talents, creativity, or special skills vital to the organization meeting its goals

- Officers, owners, and managers—includes individuals who are responsible for making decisions vital to the organization, as well as managing and motivating others

- Groups of employees—includes groups who are critically important to the organization and whose departure would leave the organization unable to function

1-3. A risk management professional for a private business must consider how an organization can survive and remain competently managed even when the owner, officers, or managers die, become disabled, or retire.

Educational Objective 2

2-1. Possible causes of personnel losses include the following:

- Death
- Disability
- Resignation, layoffs, and firing
- Retirement
- Kidnap and ransom
- War and terrorism

2-2. The various types of disability can be described as follows:

a. Temporary total disability—for a limited time, the disabled person cannot engage in any productive activity but is expected to return to work in the near future.

b. Permanent total disability—the disabled person is unable to engage in any productive work for the rest of his or her life.

c. Temporary partial disability—for a limited time, the disabled person cannot engage in all daily activities but is only partially prevented from working.

d. Permanent partial disability—the disabled person's range of activities is permanently limited, but the person can still perform many types of work.

2-3.   The main consequence of the layoff is the immediate financial cost to the organization in the form of severance pay and the possible rise in its unemployment compensation premiums, neither of which are personnel losses. A layoff would be considered a personnel loss exposure if the organization is having financial troubles and cannot afford to keep some employees even though they add value to the organization. This loss of value is the personnel loss exposure.

Educational Objective 3

3-1.   The following are four workplace hazards that can increase the frequency of personnel losses:

(1) Poor work conditions

(2) Poor compensation packages

(3) Sexual harassment

(4) Workplace violence

3-2.   An employee compensation package might include benefits such as salary, health insurance coverage, retirement and pension plans, disability insurance coverage, educational reimbursement, vacation time, fitness facilities, elder and child care services, vision and dental coverage, and stock options. Attracting and retaining quality employees is directly related to the compensation packages offered by an organization. Compensation packages should be fair and competitive to help minimize personnel losses.

3-3.   The 1991 Civil Rights Act changed the burden of proof regarding sexual harassment. Employees no longer have to suffer economic losses to collect compensation under a sexual harassment complaint. Now an employee only needs to show a hostile work environment to collect compensatory and/or punitive damages for sexual harassment in the workplace. The 1991 Act increased the sexual harassment hazard in the workplace, which leads to, among other things, higher rates of resignation.

Educational Objective 4

4-1.   The following are four financial consequences of personnel losses:

(1) Loss of the value the employee contributed to the organization

(2) Replacement costs

(3) Losses to the organization's value caused by negative publicity

(4) Losses caused by low morale

4-2.   In handling a temporary loss of an individual employee, a risk management professional should assess the length of time the person will be absent and whether a replacement can be found, the ease of replacing the person, the costs to find and train a suitable replacement, the cost in extra expenses and reduction in revenue until the replacement reaches the same level of competence, the costs added to the payroll, and the costs to reinstate the employee.

In handling a permanent loss of an individual employee, a risk management professional should assess whether the operations need to be altered, the ease and cost of finding a successor, the amount of training necessary to reach the predecessor's competence level, and the payroll cost for a replacement.

4-3. The following are the financial consequences common to all causes of personnel loss:
- Replacement costs—including recruiting, interviewing, and training costs
- Need for a succession plan
- Negative publicity
- Reduced productivity

Educational Objective 5

5-1. The strength of using risk assessment questionnaires is that the questions are universally relevant in identifying an organization's personnel loss exposures. The weakness in using risk assessment questionnaires is that they cannot uncover all loss exposures characteristic to a specific industry or organization.

5-2. An organization's loss histories might provide the following types of information:
- Mortality and disability rates
- Retirement trends
- Voluntary and involuntary employee separation histories

5-3. Two insurance industry sources of information that are useful to a risk management professional in assessing an organization's potential personnel losses are as follows:
(1) Mortality tables—which provide information regarding death rates. Assuming no adverse selection, the larger the organization, the closer its mortality rates will be to the applicable mortality table.
(2) Morbidity tables—which provide information regarding the frequency of illness.

Educational Objective 6

6-1. The types of demographic trends that might help risk management professionals forecast personnel losses include the following:
- Trends that affect morbidity
- Trends that affect mortality
- Trends that affect retirement
- Trends that affect employee separations
- Increasing age of the population

6-2. The increasing age of the population may affect organizations as follows:
- Increased labor costs caused by demand for higher salaries from experienced employees
- Difficulty in replacing intellectual capital of retired employees
- Difficulty recruiting and retaining quality employees
- Increased retirement

6-3. Employee education programs might result in fewer voluntary resignations because employees are more willing to stay with a company that helps pay for advanced degrees. The migration of the population to warmer climates might result in an increasing number of early retirements.

6-4.   a.   Glass Art, Inc., might ask itself the following questions in determining the effect of losing key employees:

- What would it do if Martin Boyer or Tony Corley were suddenly not available?
- What would be the resulting effect of this person's unavailability on achieving the organization's fundamental objectives?

    b.   Glass blowing involves melting glass rods using a furnace. There is a possibility that gas used for fuel could cause an explosion leading to the death or disability of the glass blowers. If such an event were to occur, it is possible that Glass Art, Inc., would lose not only its master glass blowers but also the most likely pool of talented people who could replace them.

    c.   Glass Art might make sure that Martin and Tony are happy with the workplace conditions that Glass Art provides. For example, Glass Art should ensure a safe, comfortable work environment as well as make sure that Martin and Tony have desirable compensation packages.

6-5.   a.   Sheila can look at the 20 percent drop in production during Bill's recovery from back surgery to determine what the financial consequences of Bill's retirement may be. She has to take account of the fact that the recovery from surgery was a temporary loss and the fact that retirement is a permanent loss. Sheila may believe that the 20 percent reduction in production would be permanent if Bill were to retire, or she may believe that the percentage reduction was so high because Bill's temporary replacement (during the recovery) was not adequate and that a permanent replacement may only cost them a few percentage points in production.

    b.   The most relevant method of assessing personnel risks that Sheila could use would be the loss histories associated with Bill's recovery from surgery. Sheila can look back through the bakery's loss records to determine when Bill has missed time from work and how it affected production during those time periods.

    c.   As a majority of the bakery's workers are college students, the main trends of concern would be trends that affect the students. Is there any trend in applications at the school? Are there fewer students attending the college? Are fewer college students working to support themselves in school?

Direct Your Learning

Assessing Net Income Loss Exposures

Educational Objectives

After learning the content of this assignment, you should be able to:

1. Explain how business risk and hazard risk can result in net income losses.

2. Describe the three types of loss exposures that can lead to a net income loss.

3. Explain how property losses, to an organization's property or other's property, can lead to net income losses.

4. Describe the financial consequences of net income losses stemming from business interruption.

5. Explain how the following methods help risk management professionals assess net income loss exposures:

   a. Risk assessment questionnaires

   b. Loss histories

   c. Financial statements and underlying accounting records

   d. Other records and documents

   e. Flowcharts and organizational charts

   f. Personal inspections

   g. Expertise within and beyond the organization

6. Given a case, analyze the income statement to measure net income loss exposures.

7. Define or describe each of the Key Words and Phrases for this assignment.

Study Materials

Required Reading:
▶ Risk Assessment
  • Chapter 10

Study Aids:
▶ SMART Online Practice Exams
▶ SMART Study Aids
  • Review Notes and Flash Cards—Assignment 10

Outline

▶ **Business Risk**

  A. General Business Risk

  B. Organization-Specific Business Risk

▶ **Hazard Risk**

  A. Property Loss Exposures

    1. Damage to the Organization's Property

    2. Damage to the Property of Others

  B. Liability Loss Exposures

  C. Personnel Loss Exposures

▶ **Financial Consequences of Business Interruption**

  A. Length of Business Interruption

    1. Small Physical Damage Loss, Long Business Interruption

    2. Seasonal Fluctuations

  B. Degree of Business Interruption

  C. Changes in Revenues

    1. Revenue From Sales

    2. Sales Value of Production

    3. Anticipated Return on Investments

  D. Changes in Expenses

    1. Continuing Expenses

    2. Extra Expenses

  E. Restoration to Normal Income

▶ **Methods of Assessing Net Income Loss Exposures**

  A. Risk Assessment Questionnaires

  B. Loss Histories

  C. Financial Statements and Underlying Accounting Records

    1. Income Statement

    2. Alternative Form of the Income Statement

    3. Relationship Among Production, Cost, and Net Income

    4. Other Financial Statements

    5. Net Income Loss Comparison

  D. Other Records and Documents

  E. Flowcharts and Organizational Charts

  F. Personal Inspections

  G. Expertise Within and Beyond the Organization

▶ **Summary**

Writing notes as you read your materials will help you remember key pieces of information.

For each assignment, you should define or describe each of the Key Words and Phrases and answer each of the Review and Application Questions.

Educational Objective 1
Explain how business risk and hazard risk can result in net income losses.

Review Questions

1-1. Explain why net income loss exposure pre-loss analysis is often challenging to a risk management professional. (p. 10.3)

1-2. Describe two main business risks to net income. (p. 10.4)

1-3. Describe the following types of business risk:

a. General business risk (p. 10.4)

b. Organization-specific business risk (pp. 10.4–10.5)

1-4. Describe and give examples of hazard risk that can cause net income losses. (p. 10.7)

Application Question

1-5. Describe how a social event, such as the Super Bowl, can positively and negatively affect an organization and its net income exposures.

Educational Objective 2

Describe the three types of loss exposures that can lead to a net income loss.

Review Questions

2-1. Identify three types of loss exposures that can cause a net income loss. (p. 10.7)

2-2. Describe and give examples of direct and indirect costs resulting from liability loss claims. (p. 10.10)

2-3.   Explain when a personel loss causes a net income loss. (p. 10.12)

Educational Objective 3

Explain how property losses, to an organization's property or other's property, can lead to net income losses.

Key Word or Phrase

Contingent net income loss exposure (p. 10.8)

Review Questions

3-1.   How can damage to an organization's property at its own premises lead to a net income loss? (p. 10.7)

3-2.   Describe how an organization might suffer a net income loss resulting from a loss of intangible property. (p. 10.8)

3-3. How might an organization suffer a net income loss through damage to the property of others? (pp. 10.8–10.10)

Educational Objective 4
Describe the financial consequences of net income losses stemming from business interruption.

Key Words and Phrases
Sales value of production (p. 10.17)

Extra expenses (p. 10.23)

Expediting expenses (p. 10.23)

Review Questions

4-1. Identify the five factors that affect the severity of a net income loss. (pp. 10.12–10.13)

4-2. Identify the techniques used to determine changes in revenue in a business interruption sustained by a mercantile business, a manufacturing business, and an investor. (p. 10.17)

4-3. Describe the following types of expenses that affect the severity of an organization's net income loss after an accident:

a. Continuing expenses (p. 10.19)

b. Extra expenses (p. 10.23)

Educational Objective 5

Explain how the following methods help risk management professionals assess net income loss exposures:

a.　Risk assessment questionnaires

b.　Loss histories

c.　Financial statements and underlying accounting records

d.　Other records and documents

e.　Flowcharts and organizational charts

f.　Personal inspections

g.　Expertise within and beyond the organization

Review Questions

5-1.　Describe the three primary financial statements used to assess net income loss exposures. (pp. 10.32–10.35)

5-2.　Explain the breakeven sales point, why it is important, and how it is calculated. (p. 10.37)

5-3.　Identify information that a risk management professional might find useful in assessing net income loss exposures from the following records and documents: (pp. 10.40–10.41)

　　a.　Board of directors minutes

b. Public information

c. Trade associations

5-4. Describe the types of information a risk management professional might obtain using the following resources:

a. Risk assessment questionnaires (p. 10.25)

b. Loss histories (p. 10.30)

c. Flowcharts and organizational charts (p. 10.41)

d. Expertise within and beyond the organization
(pp. 10.41–10.42)

Educational Objective 6

Given a case, analyze the income statement to measure net income loss exposures.

Application Questions

6-1.   High End TV and Stereo sells audio and visual equipment
to the residential market. The TV and stereo equipment it
sells usually incorporates cutting-edge technology and is very
expensive. For each of the scenarios below, determine whether
the situation is more closely related to business risk or hazard
risk, what type of loss is likely to result, and whether it will
likely generate a net income loss.

a. High End's delivery van is involved in a minor accident
while delivering a TV to a client. No injuries resulted from
the accident, but the TV being delivered was damaged.

b. High End's showroom was destroyed by a fire.

c. High End is named in a class action lawsuit by former clients who accuse High End of advertising cutting-edge technology but selling them inferior equipment that did not conform to the advertised specifications.

d. A competitor has opened a showroom directly across the street from High End and is selling the same equipment cheaper.

e. High End's most productive sales representative has resigned and is working across the street for the competitor.

f. High End's supplier of its most popular TV has suffered a major flood at its only production facility and will be closed for six months.

6-2. Risk management professionals differ on when an organization suffering a net income loss that has lasted several months has returned to its "normal" level of activity. Some believe that returning to normal means achieving the level of revenues that the organization was receiving just before the events that triggered the net income loss. Others believe that, if fundamental changes have occurred in an organization's operating environment during the period it has been shut down, an organization has returned to normal when it achieves the level of revenues that it would have been generating under these changed conditions had the event causing the net income loss not occurred.

Below is the typical monthly income statement of Jones Hardware Store for each of the eight months preceding a fire that forced complete shutdown of the store for six months. During this six months, the store would probably have experienced revenues increasing at 2 percent per month, and the costs of goods sold rising at 1 percent per month. If the store's owner believes that the store has returned to normal operations when it reaches the level of revenues and profits that reflects changes in sales and costs that would have occurred during its six-month shutdown, what would the store's normal monthly income statement have shown as its net profit for its first month after reopening? Present calculations to support your answer.

Sales	$80,000
Cost of Goods Sold	(40,000)
Other Expenses	(15,000)
Net Profit	$25,000

Answers to Assignment 10 Questions

NOTE: These answers are provided to give students a basic understanding of acceptable types of responses. They often are not the only valid answers and are not intended to provide an exhaustive response to the questions.

Educational Objective 1

1-1. Net income loss pre-loss analysis is often challenging to a risk management professional because of the difficulty in projecting the effects that a direct loss will have on an organization's revenues or expenses.

1-2. Two main business risks to net income are as follows:

(1) Price risk—the unanticipated variability in the cost of a product's input or in the product's output price

(2) Production risk—the unanticipated variability in the product's production level

1-3. a. General business risk—a risk that affects all organizations and that often results from changes in information, attitudes, technology, or general economic conditions

b. Organization-specific business risk—a risk that affects a single or small group of organizations

1-4. A hazard risk is a risk that can result in losses but no gains. Hazard risks can include direct or indirect losses resulting from industrial accidents, fires, work stoppages, or employee dishonesty.

1-5. Social events such as the Super Bowl can benefit organizations that deal with the influx of visitors to an area; for example, by increased revenue for food vendors, restaurants, hotels, and transportation services. In contrast, the event might create net income losses for manufacturing or business-to-business related services that experience lost productivity caused by the influx of traffic and security issues.

Educational Objective 2

2-1. The following are three types of loss exposures that can cause a net income loss:

(1) Property loss exposures

(2) Liability loss exposures

(3) Personnel loss exposures

2-2. Direct costs resulting from liability claims are generally considered liability losses and might include defense costs, verdicts or negotiated settlements, and the costs of complying with any injunction.

Indirect costs resulting from liability loss claims are generally considered net income losses and might include loss of reputation or market share, which could reduce revenues or increase expenses.

2-3. A personnel loss can cause a net income loss if the loss of the key employee causes the organization to lose revenue or incur extra expenses.

Educational Objective 3

3-1. Damage to an organization's property at it's own premises can lead to a net income loss if the damage prevents the organization from operating or reduces its capacity to operate.

3-2.   Intangible property includes licenses, permits, copyrights, patents, trademarks, and service marks that confer commercially valuable legal rights to their holders. A net income loss might result if the loss of intangible property reduces the value of an organization's exclusive rights or if it allows competitors to share the market and revenue that the property holder enjoyed before the intangible property loss. Legal and other expenses incurred to defend the rights also may cause a net income loss.

3-3.   An organization might suffer a net income loss through damage to the property of others in the following ways:

- Damage to other businesses on which the organization depends—damage to key suppliers, key buyers, or leader properties might result in an organization's net income loss.

- Acts of civil authorities—damage to a nearby property might create a hazardous exposure resulting in local authorities prohibiting access to the organization's property.

- Damage interrupting utility services—loss of power or other utilities might cause a shutdown of the organization's property.

Educational Objective 4

4-1.   The five factors that affect the severity of a net income loss are as follows:

(1) Length of business interruption

(2) Degree of business interruption

(3) Changes in revenues

(4) Changes in expenses

(5) Restoration to normal income

4-2.   A risk management professional uses the following bases to determine changes in revenue:

- Mercantile business—projected revenue from sales

- Manufacturing business—sales value of production

- Investor—anticipated return on investments

4-3.   a.   Continuing expenses are expenses that continue even when an organization's operations are shut down or impaired as a result of a business interruption. Expenses might include payroll; utilities; services performed by independent contractors; leases, rents, or mortgages; taxes; advertising; franchise and license fees and royalties; professional fees; insurance premiums; and depreciation.

b.   Extra expenses are incurred by an organization in order to remain in operation and to continue to provide its goods or services. Extra expenses might include rental costs of substitute buildings and equipment; excess transportation charges; employee's travel expenses to a new site; advertising and public relations expenses; and additional costs of materials.

Educational Objective 5

5-1.   The three primary financial statements used to assess net income loss exposures are as follows:

(1) Income statement—shows the organization's total revenues and expenses for a specific time period

(2) Balance sheet—shows the organization's assets and liabilities owed at a point in time

(3) Statement of cash flows—tracks revenues and expenditures over a specific time period

5-2. The breakeven sales point is a mathematical formula used to estimate the level of sales at which an organization breaks even and is used to assess the effect of a reduction in sales. It is calculated by dividing fixed coats by the contribution margin (the portion of each sales dollar that is left over after paying variable costs).

5-3. A risk management professional might find the following information useful in assessing net income loss exposures:

a. Board of directors minutes—the minutes might reveal plans to change products, production processes, or key customers or suppliers that might affect future normal streams of revenues or expenses.

b. Public information—information regarding input prices or product demand can be used to estimate potential changes in net income that arise from general business risk. Information regarding interest rates, commodity prices, inflation rates, and credit levels can be helpful in evaluating interest rate risk.

c. Trade associations—offer information for a fee, including cost of risk surveys, insurance industry financial information, and industry-specific information that can be useful in assessing general business risks.

5-4. a. Risk assessment questionnaires—aid in developing a historical perspective on net income loss exposures and serve as a starting point for assessing the potential severity of business interruptions from hazard risk.

b. Loss histories—while loss histories are more useful as measures of potential frequency than as measures of potential severity, they can still be used to assess potential severity of an organization's net income loss from current events. Records of the severity of past net income losses can help estimate the size of potential net income losses from similar occurrences.

c. Flowcharts and organizational charts—aid in assessing the effect of business interruptions on an organization's net income by identifying process bottlenecks, critical processes, and key personnel.

d. Expertise within and beyond the organization—internal resources such as accountants, attorneys, finance department staff, budgeting personnel, and operations and line managers provide information that aids in assessing net income losses. External resources such as industry experts and consultants add supplemental information.

Educational Objective 6

6-1. a. Situation is related to a hazard risk—it caused a property loss to High End's property away from its location and possibly a liability loss for the damage to property of the others involved in the accident, and more than likely would not generate a net income loss.

b. Situation is related to a hazard risk—it caused a property loss to High End's property at its location and will generate a net income loss depending on the time it takes to repair or replace the showroom.

c. Situation is related to a hazard risk—it will cause a liability loss to High End and will generate a net income loss because it will damage its reputation and cost it future sales.

   d.   Situation is related to a business risk—it will generate a net income loss because it will cost it future sales.

   e.   Situation is related to a hazard risk—it will cause a personnel loss to High End and will generate a net income loss because it will cost it future sales.

   f.   Situation is related to a hazard risk—it caused a property loss to one of High End's suppliers (damage to property of others), and would generate a net income loss if the supplier cannot supply the popular TVs that High End sells.

6-2.   The first month after reopening is the seventh month after the date of the monthly income statement figures given in the question. Therefore, the sales and the costs of goods sold amounts should be adjusted by their respective compound monthly growth factors for this seven-month period. Consequently, for the seventh month, the sales are as follows:

$$\text{Sales} = \$80,000 \times (1.02)^7$$
$$= \$80,000 \times 1.149$$
$$= \$91,920.*$$

Similarly for the seventh month, the cost of goods sold is:

$$\text{Cost of goods sold} = \$40,000 \times (1.01)^7$$
$$= \$40,000 \times 1.072$$
$$= \$42,880.*$$

* Rounded

Since Jones's other expenses each month are presumed to remain at $15,000 per month when the store reopens, its seventh-month income statement should appear as follows:

Sales	$91,920
Cost of Goods Sold	(42,880)
Other Expenses	(15,000)
	$34,040

(or comparable answers resulting from reasonable rounding).

Direct Your Learning

Understanding Forecasting

Educational Objectives

After learning the content of this assignment, you should be able to:

1. Explain why loss forecasts are important to organizations, risk management professionals, and the risk management process.

2. Explain how relevant, complete, consistent, and organized loss data are developed and why such data are important.

3. Explain probability distributions and their characteristics.

4. Contrast theoretical and empirical probability distributions.

5. Use the standard deviation of a normal probability distribution to calculate probabilities based on integer values (whole numbers) of standard deviations.

6. Describe the risk management significance of trend analysis and the two methods of trending loss data.

7. Given a case, analyze past data using the appropriate forecasting technique to project the expected value of the accidental losses that an organization will incur during a given time period.

8. Define or describe each of the Key Words and Phrases for this assignment.

Study Materials

Required Reading:
▶ Risk Assessment
  • Chapter 11

Study Aids:
▶ SMART Online Practice Exams
▶ SMART Study Aids
  • Review Notes and Flash Cards—Assignment 11

Outline

▶ **Data on Past Losses**

  A. Relevant Data

  B. Complete Data

  C. Consistent Data

    1. Consistent Basis for Data Collection

    2. Amounts of Loss Adjusted for Price Level Changes

  D. Organized Data

▶ **Probability Analysis**

  A. The Nature of Probability

  B. Data Sources for Calculating Empirical Probabilities

  C. Probability Distributions

    1. Empirical Probability Distributions

    2. Law of Large Numbers

    3. Continuous Probability Distributions

  D. Characteristics of Probability Distributions

    1. Skewness

    2. Central Tendency

    3. Dispersion

  E. Normal Distribution

▶ **Trend Analysis**

  A. Time Trends

  B. Regression Analysis

▶ **Summary**

Before starting a new assignment, briefly review the Educational Objectives of those preceding it.

For each assignment, you should define or describe each of the Key Words and Phrases and answer each of the Review and Application Questions.

Educational Objective 1

Explain why loss forecasts are important to organizations, risk management professionals, and the risk management process.

Key Word or Phrase

Forecast (p. 11.3)

Review Questions

1-1.   The risk management professional develops forecasts of future losses during which step in the risk management process? (p. 11.3)

1-2.   How does an organization use forecasts of future losses? (p. 11.3)

1-3.   How do forecasts of future losses help risk management professionals? (p. 11.3)

Educational Objective 2

Explain how relevant, complete, consistent, and organized loss data are developed and why such data are important.

Key Word or Phrase

Price index (p. 11.7)

Review Questions

2-1.   Describe the relevant data used by a risk management professional to project future losses for property, liability, personnel, and net income losses. (p. 11.4)

2-2.   What data, in addition to loss amounts, are valuable to a risk management professional in finding patterns in past losses? (p. 11.4)

2-3.   Identify two ways data must be consistent to be valuable to a risk management professional in finding patterns of past losses. (p. 11.5)

2-4. Describe how a risk management professional might organize
loss data to effectively project an organization's future losses.
(p. 11.9)

Educational Objective 3
Explain probability distributions and their characteristics.

Key Words and Phrases
Probability analysis (p. 11.10)

Probability distribution (p. 11.10)

Skewness (p. 11.18)

Symmetrical distribution (p. 11.18)

Skewed (p. 11.19)

Central tendency (p. 11.20)

Expected value (p. 11.20)

Mean (p. 11.20)

Median (p. 11.21)

Mode (p. 11.24)

Dispersion (p. 11.24)

Standard deviation (p. 11.25)

Coefficient of variation (p. 11.28)

Review Questions

3-1.   What is contained in a properly constructed probability
distribution? (p. 11.12)

3-2.   Describe how the following probability distribution characteristics describe distributions:

a. Skewness (pp. 11.18–11.19)

b. Central tendency (p. 11.20)

c. Dispersion (pp. 11.24–11.25)

3-3.   Distinguish between the following two methods of measuring
the variability among values of a data set (dispersion):

a. Standard deviation (pp. 11.25–11.26)

b. Coefficient of variation (p. 11.28)

Educational Objective 4

Contrast theoretical and empirical probability distributions.

Review Questions

4-1. Describe the following two methods of developing probability
distributions: (p. 11.11)

a. Theoretical

b. Empirical

4-2. Describe the factors that contribute to reliable empirical
probabilities and the sources of data used by risk management
professionals in calculating them. (p. 11.12)

4-3. What three criteria must events being forecasted meet in order
for the law of large numbers to apply? (p. 11.17)

Educational Objective 5

Use the standard deviation of a normal probability distribution to calculate probabilities based on integer values (whole numbers) of standard deviations.

Key Word or Phrase

Normal distribution (p. 11.28)

Review Questions

5-1.   Using a normal distribution, if 34.13 percent of all outcomes are within one standard deviation above the mean, what percentage of all outcomes are within one standard deviation above or below the mean? Explain. (p. 11.29)

5-2.   What percentage of outcomes are within two standard deviations of the mean of a normal distribution? (p. 11.29)

5-3.   What is the relationship between the mean, median, and mode of a normal distribution? (p. 11.30)

Educational Objective 6
Describe the risk management significance of trend analysis and the two methods of trending loss data.

Key Words and Phrases
Trend analysis (p. 11.31)

Trend line (p. 11.31)

Regression analysis (p. 11.33)

Dependent variable (p. 11.33)

Independent variable (p. 11.33)

Linear regression analysis (p. 11.33)

▶▶

Review Questions

6-1. Explain why a risk management professional might use trend analysis. (p. 11.31)

6-2. Describe two methods of trending loss data. (pp. 11.32–11.33)

6-3. What two aspects of interpreting linear regressions must be recognized by a risk management professional? (p. 11.35)

Educational Objective 7

Given a case, analyze past data using the appropriate forecasting technique to project the expected value of the accidental loss that an organization will incur in a given time period.

Application Questions

7-1. The following table contains the total amount paid in workers' compensation claims for the last ten years for Barnley, a medium-sized manufacturing firm.

Year	WC Claim Paid
1	$352,256
2	$400,000
3	$256,187
4	$375,898
5	$500,784
6	$475,394
7	$450,587
8	$460,578
9	$455,872
10	$501,556

a. Why should Barnley consider trying to forecast what the total amount paid in workers' compensation claims will be next year?

b. Are the data in a useable form for forecasting? If not, what needs to be done to the data so that they can be more useable?

c. Should Barnley use probability analysis or trending for forecasting?

7-2. The risk management professional of a multi-location ice cream parlor determined that, over the past five years, the firm suffered the following annual losses to inventories of cones exposed to high humidity:

Year 1 $ 2,000

Year 2   300

Year 3   10,000

Year 4   700

Year 5   2,500

a. Array these losses by dollar amount.

b. Calculate the mean, or expected, annual loss.

c. Calculate the standard deviation of these losses.

d. Calculate the coefficient of variation of these losses.

7-3.   The average bag of peat moss produced in a particular factory weighs fifty pounds. Over a three-month period, it is determined that the standard deviation in the normally distributed weight of these bags is one pound.

a. What is the probability that a randomly selected bag will weigh forty-eight pounds or less?

b. What is the probability that a randomly selected bag will weigh at least forty-nine pounds but not more than fifty-one pounds?

c. What is the probability that a randomly selected bag will weigh at least forty-eight pounds but not more than fifty-one pounds?

d. Of 10,000 bags, how many would probably weigh more than 51 pounds?

7-4. a. Refer to Exhibit 11-18 in the text. According to this exhibit, what losses should be projected for Year 9 using the linear time trend? Show your calculations.

b. Change the number of losses in Column 2 of Exhibit 11-19 to read 8, 12, 16, and 20. Recalculate Columns 3 and 4. Also recalculate the *a* and *b* values for the trend line with these new numbers of losses.

Answers to Assignment 11 Questions

NOTE: These answers are provided to give students a basic understanding of acceptable types of responses. They often are not the only valid answers and are not intended to provide an exhaustive response to the questions.

Educational Objective 1

1-1. The risk management professional develops forecasts of future losses during the second step of the risk management process—analyzing loss exposures.

1-2. An organization uses forecasts of future losses to help management make cost-effective risk management decisions.

1-3. Forecasts help risk management professionals determine the benefits and costs of each risk management alternative and choose the techniques with the greatest benefits over costs.

Educational Objective 2

2-1. The relevant data used by a risk management professional to project future losses are as follows:

- Property losses—repair or replacement cost of the property at the time it is to be restored
- Liability losses—details of claims paid and the costs of investigating, defending, or settling those claims
- Personnel and net income losses—reductions in revenue from disruptions of operations and expenses incurred while trying to return the business to normalcy

2-2. In addition to loss amounts, the following data is valuable to a risk management professional in finding patterns in past losses:

- Affected employee's experience and training
- Time of day the damage or breakdown occurred
- Task being performed
- Supervisor on duty at the time of loss

2-3. Data must be consistent in the following two ways to be valuable to a risk management professional in finding patterns of past losses:

(1) Collected on a consistent basis

(2) Expressed in constant dollars to adjust for price-level changes

2-4. A risk management professional might organize loss data in an array by size to develop loss severity distributions or loss trends in order to effectively project an organization's future losses.

Educational Objective 3

3-1. A properly constructed probability distribution always contains outcomes that are both mutually exclusive and collectively exhaustive. The sum of the probabilities must be 1.0.

3-2. The following probability distribution characteristics are used to describe distributions:

  a. Skewness is a measure of whether a distribution is symmetrical. A distribution can be symmetrical, negatively skewed, or positively skewed. If a distribution is symmetrical (balanced), the probabilities of less likely outcomes decline at the same rate on both sides of the distribution. If a distribution is negatively skewed, the most frequent outcomes are clustered on the right, and low probability is skewed left. If a distribution is positively skewed, the most frequent outcomes are clustered on the left, and low probability is skewed right.

  b. Central tendency is representative of all of the possible outcomes of the distribution. The most widely accepted representative outcomes are the expected value or mean (numeric average), the median (midpoint), and the mode (most frequent).

  c. Dispersion is a measure of variability from a distribution's mean. The variability, or scatter, among the values is measured using standard deviation and coefficient of variation.

3-3. The two methods of measuring the variability among values of a data set are as follows:

  a. Standard deviation—useful in comparing variability of distributions that have the same mean. The distribution with the largest standard deviation has the greatest variability.

  b. Coefficient of variation—useful in comparing the variability of distributions that have different shapes, means, or standard deviations. The distribution with the largest coefficient of variation has the greatest relative variability.

Educational Objective 4

4-1. The following methods are used in developing probability distributions:

  a. Theoretical probabilities are based on theoretical principles rather than actual experience and are constant as long as the physical conditions that generate them remain unchanged.

  b. Empirical probabilities are developed from historical data and are estimates whose accuracy depends on the size and representative nature of the samples being studied.

4-2. Reliability of empirical probabilities increase when they are calculated using a substantial volume of data on past losses and when the organization faces fairly stable operations so that patterns of past losses presumably will continue in the future. Sources of data include an organization's own loss data, data on the combined experience of other organizations, loss experience from regional or nationwide insurers, and loss data from organizations such as the National Safety Council and the National Fire Protection Association.

4-3. Three criteria that events being forecasted must meet for the law of large numbers to apply are as follows:

  (1) The events have occurred in the past under substantially identical conditions and have resulted from unchanging, basic causal forces.

  (2) The events can be expected to occur in the future under the same unchanging conditions.

  (3) The events have been, and will continue to be, both independent of one another and sufficiently numerous.

Educational Objective 5

5-1. In a normal distribution with 34.13 percent of all outcomes falling within one standard deviation above the mean, a total of 68.26 percent of all outcomes are within one standard deviation above or below the mean. This is true because every normal distribution is symmetrical.

5-2. 95.44 percent of all possible outcomes are within two standard deviations of the mean of a normal distribution.

5-3. The normal distribution is a symmetrical distribution. Therefore, the mean, median, and mode are all the same value.

Educational Objective 6

6-1. A risk management professional might use trend analysis to improve the forecasting of future losses. Trend analysis looks for predictable patterns in a changing environment and adjusts loss data for anticipated changes in factors presumed to affect the frequency or severity of accidental losses.

6-2. Two methods of trending loss data are as follows:

(1) Time trends—loss data are charted on a linear time period, and a trend line is drawn to indicate a loss frequency trend.

(2) Regression analysis—a statistical technique that is used to estimate relationships between dependent variables (variables being forecasted) and independent variables (variables that determine the value of the dependent variable).

6-3. Two aspects of interpreting linear regressions are as follows:

(1) A linear regression line might not be accurate when it gets very far away from the actual data values used.

(2) The dependent variable's value calculated by the linear regression is not likely to exactly equal the historical value for that past year.

Educational Objective 7

7-1. a. Barnley should consider forecasting next year's workers' compensation costs to aid in the budgeting process and to ensure that the organization understands the costs and benefits of the various risk management techniques that can be used to control or finance workers' compensation loss exposures.

b. It is not clear from the data that they are relevant, complete, consistent, or organized. It appears that the data are relevant, using past workers' compensation costs to predict future costs. However, only the total cost is listed; other information that may be useful to make the data complete, such as the number of employees or man-hours worked, is not included. Furthermore, it is not clear if the data are reported in constant dollars to make them consistent. Finally, as only aggregate claims are listed, it is not clear how organized the data are.

c. If the number of employees (or man-hours) was consistent, probability analysis could be used. However, trending could be used if one or more relevant factors were changing over time.

7-2. a. Dollar amount array: $300; $700; $2,000; $2,500; $10,000

b. Mean = ($300 + $700 + $2,000 + $2,500 + $10,000) ÷ 5

= $15,500 ÷ 5

= $3,100.

c.

Loss (× $1,000)	Deviation From Mean (3.1)	Squared Deviation
2.0	−1.1	1.21
0.3	−2.8	7.84
10.0	6.9	47.61
0.7	−2.4	5.76
2.5	−0.6	0.36
		62.78

$$\text{Standard Deviation} = \sqrt{(62.78 \div 4)}$$
$$= \sqrt{15.695}$$
$$= 3.962.$$

(Note: Answer expressed in square root form is sufficient.)

d. Coefficient of variation = standard deviation ÷ mean

= 3.962 ÷ 3.1

= 1.278.

7-3. a. p(48 or less) = p(more than 2 standard deviations below mean)

= .5000 − (.3413 + .1359)

= .0228.

b. p(49 to 51) = p(1 standard deviation above or below mean)

= .3413 + .3413

= .6826.

c. p(48 to 51) = p(2 standard deviations below to 1 standard deviation above mean)

= .4772 + .3413

= .8185.

d. p(51 or more) = p(more than 1 standard deviation above mean)

= .5000 − .3413

= .1587.

10,000 bags × 0.1587 = 1,587 bags.

7-4. a. Y (losses) $= 3 + .7x$

if $x = 9$,

$Y = 3 + (9 \times .7)$

$= 3 + 6.3$

$= 9.3$ (9 or 10, since fractional losses are impossible).

b.

Years	**Losses**		
x	y	xy	x^2
1	8	8	1
2	12	24	4
3	16	48	9
4	20	80	16
10	56	160	30

$a = \dfrac{(56)(30) - (10)(160)}{4(30) - (10)^2}$

$= \dfrac{1680 - 1600}{20}$

$= 4.0.$

$b = \dfrac{4(160) - (10)(56)}{4(30) - (10)^2}$

$= \dfrac{640 - 560}{20}$

$= 4.0.$

Direct Your Learning

Applying Forecasting

Educational Objectives

After learning the content of this assignment, you should be able to:

1. Calculate the joint probability of the following:

   a. Two or more independent events

   b. Two or more dependent events

   c. Two or more sequential events

   d. Two or more events not occurring

2. Calculate the alternative probability of the following:

   a. Two mutually exclusive events

   b. Two nonmutually exclusive events

3. Calculate trend lines showing the following:

   a. Combined effects of two or more trends that can properly be added

   b. Constant percentage rate of change

4. Define or describe each of the Key Words and Phrases for this assignment.

Study Materials

Required Reading:
▶ Risk Assessment
  • Chapter 12

Study Aids:
▶ SMART Online
  Practice Exams
▶ SMART Study Aids
  • Review Notes and
    Flash Cards—
    Assignment 12

Outline

▶ **Applied Calculations Involving Probabilities**

A. Basic Notation

B. Joint Probabilities

    1. Independent Events

    2. Dependent Events

    3. Sequential Events

    4. Other Joint Probability Calculations

C. Alternative Probabilities

    1. Mutually Exclusive Events

    2. Nonmutually Exclusive Events

▶ **Applied Trend Analysis**

A. Combining Trends—Defining the Model

    1. First Independent Variable: Ton-Miles

    2. Second Independent Variable: Freight Rates

B. An Illustrative Forecast

▶ **Summary**

Perform a final review before your exam, but don't cram. Give yourself between two and four hours to go over the course work.

For each assignment, you should define or describe each of the Key Words and Phrases and answer each of the Review and Application Questions.

Educational Objective 1

Calculate the joint probability of the following:

a. Two or more independent events

b. Two or more dependent events

c. Two or more sequential events

d. Two or more events not occurring

Key Words and Phrases

Joint probability (p. 12.5)

Conditional probability (p. 12.7)

Review Questions

1-1. Probability calculations typically use some basic notation, such as the symbol "$p(\ )$," meaning the "probability of" the event specified in the parentheses. Identify three other symbols used in probability notation and explain the meaning of each of them. (pp. 12.4–12.5)

1-2. Most probability calculations rest on two assumptions. State these two assumptions. (p. 12.5)

1-3. Calculate the probability of the following events: (p. 12.4)

    a. A five on a single roll of one die

    b. A nine on a single roll of two dice

1-4. Explain what a risk management professional needs to consider when calculating joint probabilities of sequential events. (pp. 12.7–12.8)

1-5. If the probability of the driver of a car being killed in an accident is .01, what is the probability of the driver not being killed in an accident? (p. 12.5)

Application Question

1-6. Over a period of several years, one milk truck in every twenty operated by the Quality Dairy Company has been involved in a traffic accident each year. In four out of five accidents, the driver has been unhurt. Of those drivers who have been injured or killed, seven out of ten have been injured, and three out of ten have been killed.

a. What is the probability that a designated Quality Dairy truck will:

   (1) Be involved in a traffic accident this year?

   (2) Not be involved in a traffic accident this year?

b. What is the probability that the driver of a truck involved in an accident:

   (1) Will be unhurt?

   (2) Will be either injured or killed?

(3)   Will be injured but not killed?

(4)   Will be killed?

c. What is the probability that Bill, a driver of a Quality Dairy Company truck, will within the next year:

(1)   Not be involved in an accident in a company truck?

(2)   Be involved in an accident in a company truck this year and will escape unhurt?

(3)   Be involved in an accident in a company truck and be injured, but not killed?

(4)   Be involved in an accident in a company truck and be killed?

d. Can a probability distribution on Bill's accident experience in a given year be constructed on the basis of the answers to c.(1) through c.(4)?

e. Suppose that Bill and Sam drive separate trucks for the Quality Dairy Company and that the probabilities described previously apply to each of these drivers. Is it reasonable to assume that Bill's being involved in an accident in a Company truck and Sam's being similarly involved are:

(1)   Independent events? Explain.

(2)   Mutually exclusive events? Explain.

f. If an accident involving Sam and an accident involving Bill
    are independent—but not mutually exclusive—events, what
    is the probability that, in the coming year:

    (1) Neither of them will be involved in an accident?

    (2) Both will be involved in an accident?

    (3) At least one and possibly both will be involved in an
         accident?

    (4) One but not the other will be involved in an accident?

g. Suppose that Joe is Bill's helper in operating a Quality
    Dairy Company truck and rides with Bill in the same truck
    when making deliveries and that the probabilities described
    previously apply to both men.

    (1) Is it reasonable to assume that an injury to Bill and an
         injury to Joe are independent events? Explain.

(2) Is it reasonable to assume that an injury to Bill and an injury to Joe are mutually exclusive events? Explain.

(3) What is the probability that Joe will be killed in an accident involving a company truck in the coming year?

(4) If in nine out of ten cases an accident that injures a driver also injures or kills his helper, what is the probability that if Bill is injured in a traffic accident, Joe will be unhurt?

Educational Objective 2

Calculate the alternative probability of the following:

a. Two mutually exclusive events

b. Two nonmutually exclusive events

Key Word or Phrase

Alternative probability (p. 12.9)

Review Questions

2-1.   Explain how the calculation of mutually exclusive events
and the calculation of non-mutually exclusive events differ.
Explain. (pp. 12.10–12.11)

2-2.   In one draw of one card from a standard deck containing no
jokers, calculate the following:

a. The probability of drawing a five (p. 12.9)

b. The probability of drawing a five or a jack (p. 12.10)

c. The probability of drawing a diamond or a spade (p. 12.10)

2-3.   In one draw of one card from a standard deck containing no
jokers, calculate the probability of drawing a five or a spade.
(p. 12.11)

Application Question

2-4. The All-Clean Company owns and operates a number of automatic laundries in a particular city. All-Clean's risk management professional has learned that, over the past five years, the company's expenditures for repairing broken washing or drying machines have increased as the number of machines has grown from 40 to 120. The amounts of these repair costs (in constant dollars for the current Year 5) have been as follows:

Year	Machines	Repair Costs (× $1,000)
1	40	10
2	60	15
3	90	25
4	120	30
5	120	35

All-Clean is considering selling one of its automatic laundries, which would reduce the number of machines to 95. If All-Clean were to sell this facility at the end of the current Year 5, and if the price of repairs were to increase 6 percent between Year 5 and Year 6, what would be an appropriate estimate of All-Clean's machine repair costs in Year 6?

Educational Objective 3

Calculate trend lines showing the following:

a.   Combined effects of two or more trends that can properly be added

b.   Constant percentage rate of change

Review Questions

3-1.   Briefly describe why a risk management professional may want to use trend analysis to project future accidental losses. (p. 12.14)

3-2.   In combining independent trends to project future accidental losses, why is it important to know whether the two trends are independent? (p. 12.15)

3-3.   What steps should a risk management professional take to improve linear projection trend accuracy? (p. 12.19)

▶▶

Application Question

3-4.   The warehouses of the Omega Corporation have experienced numerous vandalism losses, which are becoming increasingly expensive to repair. Assume that last year (Year 1) Omega suffered 100 vandalism losses and that the average cost of repair for each of these losses was $100. Omega's risk management professional estimates that the number of vandalism losses will increase by 10 per year and that the cost of repair for the average vandalism loss will increase by 10 percent per year.

   a. What was the dollar amount of vandalism losses last year (Year 1) in nominal dollars for last year?

   b. What is the projected dollar amount of vandalism losses for the current year (Year 2) in current year (Year 2) dollars?

   c. What will be the dollar amount of these losses in nominal dollars (Year 3 dollars) for next year (Year 3)?

   d. What will be the dollar amount of losses in nominal dollars (Year 5 dollars) in Year 5?

Answers to Assignment 12 Questions

NOTE: These answers are provided to give students a basic understanding of acceptable types of responses. They often are not the only valid answers and are not intended to provide an exhaustive response to the questions.

Educational Objective 1

1-1. Three other symbols used in probability notation are as follows:

  (1) "n" to designate the number of exposure units from which a probability is developed or to which it is applied

  (2) "m" to designate the number of occurrences of the event whose probability is sought

  (3) "$E(\ )$" to designate the expected number or the expected value

1-2. The two assumptions on which most probability calculations rest are as follows:

  (1) The probability, p, remains constant and is valid for future events whose probability is being calculated.

  (2) An event occurs or does not occur—the occurrence/nonoccurrence of an event is mutually exclusive and collectively exhaustive.

1-3. a. $\frac{1}{6}$. There are six possible outcomes, only one of which is a five.

  b. There are 36 possible combinations on the roll of two dice. There are four possible combinations of two dice that equal a total of nine. Therefore, the probability is $\frac{4}{36}$ or $\frac{1}{9}$.

Die #1	Die #2
3	6
4	5
5	4
6	3

1-4. When calculating joint probabilities of sequential events, a risk management professional needs to take great care in defining the events whose probability is being calculated. In addition, the order of the events, and whether the probability of one event changes depending on whether another event has already occurred, are critical considerations.

1-5. The probability of the driver not being killed in an accident is $1 - .01 = .99$.

1-6. a. (1) $\frac{1}{20}$ or .05

  (2) $\frac{19}{20}$ or .95

  b. (1) $\frac{4}{5}$ or .80

  (2) $\frac{1}{5}$ or .20

  (3) $\frac{1}{5} \times \frac{7}{10} = \frac{7}{50}$ or .14.

  (4) $\frac{1}{5} \times \frac{3}{10} = \frac{3}{50}$ or .06.

  c. (1) $^{19}/_{20}$ or .95.

    (2) $^{1}/_{20} \times ^{4}/_{5} = ^{4}/_{100}$ or .04.

    (3) $^{1}/_{20} \times (^{1}/_{5} \times ^{7}/_{10}) = ^{7}/_{1000}$ or .007.

    (4) $^{1}/_{20} \times ^{6}/_{100} = ^{3}/_{1000}$ or .003.

  d. Yes. See below:

Outcome	Probability
Bill not in accident	.950
Bill in accident, but not injured	.040
Bill injured in accident	.007
Bill killed in accident	.003
Total	1.000

  e. (1) Yes, except for accidents on company property or elsewhere if the two trucks are together. Otherwise the two trucks face independent hazards.

    (2) No, because one driver being in an accident does not preclude the other driver from being in an accident.

  f. (1) $^{19}/_{20} \times ^{19}/_{20} = ^{361}/_{400}$ or .9025.

    (2) $^{1}/_{20} \times ^{1}/_{20} = ^{1}/_{400}$ or .0025.

    (3) $^{1}/_{20} + ^{1}/_{20} - (^{1}/_{20} \times ^{1}/_{20}) = ^{39}/_{400}$ or .0975.

    (4) There are two mutually exclusive ways in which this result can occur: (i) Bill is in an accident, but Sam is not; (ii) Sam is in an accident, but Bill is not. The desired probability is as follows:

$$p(1) + p(2) = (^{1}/_{20})(^{19}/_{20}) + (^{19}/_{20})(^{1}/_{20})$$
$$= ^{38}/_{400}$$
$$= ^{19}/_{200} \text{ or } .095.$$

  g. (1) No, because both Bill and Joe are usually in the same truck.

    (2) No, because either Bill or Joe being in an accident does not make it impossible for the other to be in an accident.

    (3) .003

    (4) $1 - ^{9}/_{10} = ^{1}/_{10}$ or .10.

Educational Objective 2

2-1. With mutually exclusive events, the occurrence of one event makes the other event impossible. The probability that any one event will occur is the sum of their separate probabilities. With non-mutually exclusive events, two or more events can occur within a specified time period. The probability that at least one and possibly both or all of them will occur is the sum of their separate probabilities minus the joint probability that they will both or all occur.

2-2. a. The probability of drawing a five is $^{4}/_{52}$ or $^{1}/_{13}$.

  b. The probability of drawing a five or a jack is $^{1}/_{13} + ^{1}/_{13} = ^{2}/_{13}$. The events are mutually exclusive.

  c. The probability of drawing a diamond or a spade is $^{1}/_{4} + ^{1}/_{4} = ^{1}/_{2}$. The events are mutually exclusive.

2-3.   The probability of drawing a five or a spade is $\frac{4}{52} + \frac{13}{52} - \frac{1}{52} = \frac{16}{52}$ or $\frac{4}{13}$. The events are not mutually exclusive.

2-4.   If the physical volume of repairs is related to the number of machines through a regression equation, and if the price of each unit of repair work increases by 6 percent, then the overall cost of All-Clean's machine repairs in Year 6 can reasonably be projected by applying the appropriate regression equation, finding the constant-dollar amount of repairs associated with 95 machines, and increasing this amount by 6 percent to adjust for anticipated inflation in Year 6. These calculations are as follows:

Machines (× 10) (x)	Repair Costs (× \$1,000) (y)	xy	x^2
4	10	40	16
6	15	90	36
9	25	225	81
12	30	360	144
12	35	420	144
43	115	1,135	421

$$y(\times \$1,000) = -1.52 + (2.85 \times 9.5)$$

$$= 25.56 \text{ or } \$25,560 \text{ in Year 5 prices (rounded)}.$$

$$\text{Cost in Year 6 prices} = \$25,560 \times 1.06$$

$$= \$27,094 \text{ (rounded)}.$$

Educational Objective 3

3-1.   A risk management professional may want to use trend analysis to project future accidental losses because of the ability to more accurately forecast loss frequency, loss severity, or the costs of insurance or retention.

3-2.   It is important to know whether two trends are independent because combining dependent trends would yield invalid results.

3-3.   Steps a risk management professional should take to improve linear projection trend accuracy are as follows:

* Obtain as much relevant data as possible for calculating trends
* Experiment with both linear and curvilinear trending techniques
* Redraw or recalculate trend lines to incorporate new data

3-4.   a.   Last year: 100 losses at \$100 average loss = \$10,000 total losses.

b.   Current year: 110 losses at \$110 average loss = \$12,100 total losses.

c.   Next year: 120 losses at an average of \$110 × (1 + 0.10) per loss = 120 losses at \$121 average loss = \$14,520 total losses.

d.   Three years from current year: 140 losses, and the average loss will be
     $110 × [(1.10)(1.10)(1.10)] or $110 × (1.10)^3, or $110 × 1.331, or $146.41.

     140 losses × $146.41 average loss = $20,497.40 total losses.

Direct Your Learning

Understanding Cash Flow Analysis

Educational Objectives

After learning the content of this assignment, you should be able to:

1. Explain why net cash flows are important to an organization.

2. Explain why money has a "time value" and how to determine the present value.

3. Calculate the present values of future single payments or streams of future payments using present value tables.

4. Explain how to use the net present value and internal rate of return methods to evaluate capital investment proposals.

5. Apply the net present value and internal rate of return methods to rank capital investment proposals.

6. Calculate the internal rate of return for a capital investment proposal using interpolation.

7. Explain how to calculate differential annual after-tax net cash flows for an investment proposal.

8. Given a case, evaluate two investment proposals using net cash flow analysis.

9. Define or describe each of the Key Words and Phrases for this assignment.

Study Materials

Required Reading:
▶ Risk Assessment
  • Chapter 13

Study Aids:
▶ SMART Online Practice Exams
▶ SMART Study Aids
  • Review Notes and Flash Cards—Assignment 13

Outline

▶ **Importance of Net Cash Flows**

▶ **Time Value of Money**

    A. Present Value

    B. Present Value Calculations

        1. Present Payment

        2. Single Future Payment

        3. Stream of Equal Future Payments

        4. Stream of Unequal Future Payments

▶ **Methods for Evaluating Capital Investment Proposals**

    A. Net Present Value (NPV) Method

    B. Internal Rate of Return (IRR) Method

▶ **Capital Investment Proposal Ranking**

▶ **Calculation of Differential Annual After-Tax Net Cash Flows**

▶ **Summary**

▶ **Appendix A—Present Value of $1 Received at the End of a Period**

▶ **Appendix B—Present Value of $1 Received at the End of Each Period for *n* Periods**

When reviewing for your exam, remember to allot time for frequent breaks.

For each assignment, you should define or describe each of the Key Words and Phrases and answer each of the Review and Application Questions.

Educational Objective 1

Explain why net cash flows are important to an organization.

Key Words and Phrases

Net cash flow (NCF) (p. 13.3)

Capital budgeting (p. 13.4)

Operating expenditures (p. 13.4)

Capital expenditures (p. 13.4)

Review Questions

1-1. How does projecting net cash flows benefit an organization's managers? (p. 13.4)

1-2.   What are two types of expenditures disbursed by an organization?
(p. 13.4)

1-3.   Describe capital expenditures. (p. 13.4)

Educational Objective 2
Explain why money has a "time value" and how to determine the present value.

Key Words and Phrases
Time value of money (p. 13.4)

Rate of return (p. 13.5)

Present value (p. 13.5)

Opportunity cost (p. 13.5)

Cost of capital (p. 13.6)

Review Questions

2-1.   Explain the time value of money. (p. 13.4)

2-2.   Describe the two factors that determine present value.
        (pp. 13.5–13.6)

2-3.   Explain the opportunity cost of money. (p.13.5)

Educational Objective 3

Calculate the present values of future single payments or streams of future payments using present value tables.

Review Questions

3-1.   What values might be used when calculating a present value? (pp. 13.7–13.12)

3-2.   Is the present value of $1 paid in five years at a discount rate of 10 percent greater than the present value of $1 paid in five years at a discount rate of 5 percent? (p. 13.8)

3-3.   Which present value table should be used on a stream of unequal payments? (p. 13.12)

▶▶

Educational Objective 4

Explain how to use the net present value and internal rate of return methods to evaluate capital investment proposals.

Key Words and Phrases

Salvage value (p. 13.14)

Net present value (NPV) (p. 13.15)

Differential annual after-tax net cash flow (p. 13.15)

Internal rate of return (IRR) (p. 13.17)

Review Questions

4-1. Describe two evaluation methods used to apply cash flow analysis as a decision criterion. (p. 13.14)

4-2. Identify the information required to evaluate capital investment proposals. (p. 13.14)

4-3. Describe the implications of a positive net present value result of a capital investment proposal evaluation using the net present value method. (p. 13.15)

Educational Objective 5

Apply the net present value and internal rate of return methods to rank capital investment proposals.

Key Word or Phrase

Profitability index (p. 13.26)

Review Questions

5-1. When evaluating capital investment proposals, what two conditions may result in differences in rankings based on the NPV method and the IRR method? (pp. 13.23–13.26)

5-2. Describe the profitability index and how it is calculated. (p. 13.26)

5-3.   Describe acceptable capital investment proposal rankings based
        on the profitability index and explain how management uses
        rankings to evaluate proposals. (p. 13.26)

Educational Objective 6

Calculate the internal rate of return for a capital investment proposal using interpolation.

Review Questions

6-1.   What is the advantage to a risk management professional of
        calculating the IRR through interpolation? (p. 13.17)

6-2.   What is the formula used for interpolation? (p. 13.20)

6-3.   Identify the steps used to calculate the internal rate of return
        (IRR) through interpolation. (p. 13.20)

Educational Objective 7

Explain how to calculate differential annual after-tax net cash flows for an investment proposal.

Key Words and Phrases

Depreciation (p. 13.27)

Straight-line depreciation method (p. 13.27)

Review Questions

7-1.   Explain how for-profit organizations recognize income taxes in
        calculating net cash flows. (p. 13.26)

7-2.   Why must income taxes be calculated separately from other
        cash expenditures? (p. 13.26)

7-3.   Explain how depreciation is recognized in calculating cash flow
        for capital budgeting decisions. (p. 13.27)

Educational Objective 8

Given a case, evaluate two investment proposals using net cash flow analysis.

Application Questions

8-1. The Constellation Restaurant is considering the purchase of a new type of electronic oven for $40,000 that, because of its great speed, can be expected to add $15,000 to the restaurant's annual revenue during each of the ten years of the oven's estimated useful life. However, because the technology underlying this oven is so new, its maintenance and repair expenses can be expected to be $3,000 a year more than the maintenance and repair expenses for the five conventional ovens the new oven is replacing. Neither the old ovens nor the new one will have any salvage value. The restaurant management will purchase the new oven only if its after-tax internal rate of return can be expected to exceed 25 percent annually. (Note: Discounted at 25 percent interest, the present value of $1 to be received at the end of each of the next ten years is $3.57.)

    a. Assuming straight-line depreciation and a 50 percent income tax rate, should Constellation Restaurant purchase the new oven? Support your answer with appropriate calculations.

    b. Because the new technology of this oven makes breakdowns and repair costs somewhat uncertain, the projected $15,000 of additional annual revenue cannot be predicted with certainty; instead, it is represented by the following probability distribution:

Probability	Annual Additional Revenue
.10	$ 5,000
.20	10,000
.40	15,000
.15	20,000
.10	25,000
.05	30,000

According to this probability distribution, what is the expected value of the annual additional revenue from the new oven? Show your calculations.

c. If the additional revenue from the oven, instead of being $15,000 a year, is the annual expected value calculated in your answer to (b), will the after-tax internal rate of return on the oven be higher than that calculated in your answer to (a)? Briefly explain.

8-2. The Blue Corporation is purchasing a new soap machine
      for $15,400. The new machine's annual output will bring in
      $3,000 more revenue than the old machine it is replacing. The
      old machine has no salvage value; nor will the new machine
      at the end of its seven-year estimated useful life. The new
      machine costs $1,000 less per year to operate than did the old
      machine. The income tax rate is 35 percent.

      a. What is the internal rate of return to Blue Corporation on
         the new machine?

      b. Assume the $3,000 of additional annual revenue from the
         new machine is not known with certainty. If the follow-
         ing probability distribution applies to each year's additional
         revenue from the new machine, and management wants to
         make its decisions on the basis of the expected value of this
         additional revenue, will the new machine have a positive
         net present value if the minimum acceptable rate of return is
         14 percent per year compounded annually?

Probability	Additional Revenue
.10	$ 2,000
.20	3,000
.40	3,600
.15	5,000
.10	8,000
.05	10,000

c. Assume that at the end of the seven-year useful life span of the machine, the Blue Corporation's management finds that the machine did, in fact, generate the following amounts of additional revenue in the indicated years:

Year	Additional Revenue
1	$ 8,000
2	7,000
3	6,000
4	5,000
5	4,000
6	3,000
7	2,000

Discounted at 14 percent compounded interest per year, what would have been the present value in Year 0 of this actual stream of additional revenue? Show your calculations.

d. The actual annual revenues given in (c) decreased from year to year, with the highest amount in the earliest year and the lowest amount in the most distant year. If this pattern of additional revenues had been reversed—with additional revenues being $2,000 at the first year and $8,000 at the seventh year—would the present value of this stream of additional revenue be higher or lower than that calculated in (c)? Explain the reason(s) underlying your conclusions.

Answers to Assignment 13 Questions

NOTE: These answers are provided to give students a basic understanding of acceptable types of responses. They often are not the only valid answers and are not intended to provide an exhaustive response to the questions.

Educational Objective 1

1-1. Projecting net cash flows benefits an organization's managers by giving a valid financial criterion for choosing assets or activities that would provide the most financial benefit to the organization.

1-2. Two types of expenditures disbursed by an organization are operating expenditures and capital expenditures.

1-3. Capital expenditures are disbursements for assets that will be consumed over a relatively long period, usually over multiple accounting periods.

Educational Objective 2

2-1. Money received today is worth more than money received at a later date because money already received can be invested and start earning money immediately. The value of money promised for a later date cannot be invested to generate income until that later date.

2-2. The two factors that determine present value are as follows:

(1) Appropriate discount rate—the time value cost associated with the use of money, normally expressed as a percentage for each year that the money is being used

(2) Length of time before each cash flow occurs—the number of years or units of time until the cash flow(s) are received or paid

2-3. The opportunity cost of money is the rate of return that money could have earned had it been put to the best alternative use that entails comparable risk. The cost arises because selecting one use for money necessarily prevents that money from being used for some other purpose.

Educational Objective 3

3-1. The following values might be used in calculating a present value:

- Present payment—the value today of that payment
- Present value of single future payment (PV_p)—one payment at some future date, most often the salvage or resale value
- Present value of stream of equal future payments (PV_{ep})—the sum of the present values of each of the separate equal payments, often called an annuity
- Present value of stream of unequal future payments (PV_{up})—the sum of the present values of the individual payments

3-2. No. For any given period, such as five years, a higher interest or discount rate implies a lower present value.

3-3. The "Present Value of $1 Received at the End of a Period" table should be used for streams of unequal payments.

Educational Objective 4

4-1. Two evaluation methods used to apply cash flow analysis as a decision criterion are as follows:

(1) Net present value method (NPV)—calculates whether, at a specified discount rate, the present value of a proposal's net cash flow is positive or negative. A positive net cash flow means that the proposal generates a rate of return higher than the specified rate.

(2) Internal rate of return (IRR) method—calculates the discount rate at which the present value of a proposal's net cash flow is zero. If the calculated discount rate is equal to or exceeds the minimally acceptable rate, the proposal is acceptable.

4-2. The information required to evaluate capital investment proposals is as follows:

- Amount of the initial investment
- Acceptable annual rate of return
- Amount and timing of the differential (incremental) annual after-tax net cash flows associated with the proposal over its estimated useful life
- Salvage value (if any) of the investment

4-3. Any proposal whose projected cash inflows have a present value greater than the present value of the required outflows is acceptable by the NPV method.

Educational Objective 5

5-1. The two conditions that may result in differences in rankings based on the NPV method and the IRR method are as follows:

(1) The amount of the initial investment must be substantially different.

(2) Capital limitations must exist that prevent an organization from funding all acceptable proposals.

5-2. The profitability index is a method used to rank capital investment proposals and is calculated by dividing the present value of future net cash flows by the present value of the amount of the initial investment.

5-3. Acceptable capital investment proposals have a profitability index of at least 1.0. Risk management professionals should compare results obtained from a profitability ranking to those obtained by selecting proposals using total net present value and internal rate of return before accepting the proposal.

Educational Objective 6

6-1. The advantage to the risk management professional of calculating the IRR through interpolation is that it results in a more precise estimate of the IRR generated by the cash flows of the capital investment proposal.

6-2. The formula used for interpolation is as follows:

$$r = \text{Smaller discount rate} + \left[\frac{PVF(\text{calculations differences})}{PVF(\text{appendix differences})} \times \text{Discount rate differences} \right].$$

6-3.   The steps used to calculate the internal rate of return (IRR) through interpolation are as follows:

- Divide the initial investment in the proposal by the annual differential after-tax net cash flows
- Identify the two present value factors by reference to the appropriate present value factors tables
- Record both the present value factors and discount rates associated with them
- Calculate the differences and use the interpolation formula

Educational Objective 7

7-1.   For-profit organizations deduct income taxes from cash revenues in calculating net cash flows.

7-2.   Income taxes must be calculated separately from other cash expenditures because they are a percentage of taxable income, which recognizes some noncash revenues and expenses.

7-3.   In calculating cash flow for capital budgeting decisions, depreciation is not a cash outflow in the period in which the expense is recognized but rather affects cash flow calculations when the revenues and expenses result in actual cash receipt or expenditure.

Educational Objective 8

8-1.   a.   <u>Calculation of oven's annual after-tax NCF:</u>

Differential Cash Revenues		$15,000
Less: Differential Cash Expenses		
(except income taxes)		($ 3,000)
Before-Tax NCF:		$12,000
Less: Differential Income taxes:		
Before-Tax NCF:	$12,000	
Less: Differential Depreciation		
expense ($40,000 ÷ 10 years)	($ 4,000)	
Taxable Income	$ 8,000	
Income Taxes (50%)		($ 4,000)
After-Tax NCF:		$ 8,000

<u>NCF Analysis</u>

Factors:

Initial Investment	$40,000
Life of Project	10 years
Differential Annual after-tax NCF	$ 8,000
Minimum acceptable rate of return (annual)	25.00%

Analysis by NPV:

PV of differential NCF ($8,000 × 3.57)	$28,560
Less: PV of initial investment	($40,000)
NPV:	($11,440)

Analysis by NPV:

PVF = Initial Investment ÷ Differential NCF

PVF = $40,000 ÷ $8,000 = 5.000.

Interpolation to find the IRR (*r*):

Rate of Return	PVF	PVF
15.00%	5.019	
r		5.000
16.00%	4.833	
Differences: 1.00%	0.186	0.019

r = 15% + [(0.019 ÷ 0.186) × 1%]

  = 15% + 0.102%

  = 15.1%.

As the NPV is negative and the internal rate of return on the oven after taxes is less than 25%, the restaurant should not purchase a new oven.

b.

Probability	Revenue	Expected Value
.10	$ 5,000	$ 500
.20	10,000	2,000
.40	15,000	6,000
.15	20,000	3,000
.10	25,000	2,500
.05	30,000	1,500
		$15,500

c. Since the annual revenue could be higher ($15,500 versus $15,000) and other factors will presumably not change, the rate of return can be expected to be higher.

8-2.   a.   <u>Calculation of soap machine's annual after-tax NCF:</u>

Differential Cash Revenues		$3,000
Plus Reduction in Differential Cash Expenses		
(except income taxes)		$1,000
Before-Tax NCF:		$4,000
Less: Differential Income taxes:		
Before-Tax NCF:	$4,000	
Less: Differential Depreciation		
expense ($15,400 ÷ 7 years)	($2,200)	
Taxable Income	$1,800	
Income Taxes (35%)		($630)
After-Tax NCF:		$3,370

<u>NCF Analysis</u>

Factors:

Initial Investment	$15,400
Life of Project	7 years
Differential Annual after-tax NCF	$3,370
Minimum acceptable rate of return (annual)	14.00%

Analysis by IRR:

PVF = Initial Investment ÷ Differential NCF

PVF = $15,400 ÷ $3,370 = 4.570.

Interpolation to find the IRR (r):

Rate of Return	PVF	PVF
10.00%	4.868	
r		4.570
12.00%	4.564	
Differences: 2.00%	0.304	0.298

$r = 10\% + [(0.298 ÷ 0.304) × 2\%]$

  $= 10\% + 1.96\%$

  $= 11.96\%.$

b. Yes, the new machine will generate a positive NPV and acceptable rate of return, based on the following calculations:

Probability	Additional Revenue	Expected Value
.10	$ 2,000	$ 200
.20	3,000	600
.40	3,600	1,440
.15	5,000	750
.10	8,000	800
.05	10,000	500
Expected value		$4,290

Recalculation of soap machine's annual after-tax NCF:

Differential Cash Revenues		$4,290
Plus Reduction in Differential Cash Expenses		
(except income taxes)		$1,000
Before-Tax NCF:		$5,290
Less: Differential Income taxes:		
Before-Tax NCF:	$5,290	
Less: Differential Depreciation		
expense ($15,400 ÷ 7 years)	($2,200)	
Taxable Income	$3,090	
Income Taxes (35%)		($1,082)
After-Tax NCF:		$4,209

NCF Analysis

Factors:

Initial Investment	$15,400
Life of Project	7 years
Differential Annual after-tax NCF	$4,209
Minimum acceptable rate of return (annual)	14.00%

Analysis by NPV:

PV of differential NCF ($4,209 × 4.288)	$18,046
Less: PV of initial investment	($15,400)
NPV:	$ 2,646

Analysis by IRR:

PVF = Initial Investment ÷ Differential NCF

PVF = $15,400 ÷ $4,209 = 3.659.

Interpolation to find the IRR (r):

Rate of Return	PVF	PVF
18.00%	3.812	
r		3.659
20.00%	3.605	
Differences: 2.00%	0.207	0.153

$r = 18\% + [(0.153 \div 0.207) \times 2\%]$

  $= 18\% + 1.48\%$

  $= 19.48\%$.

c.

Year	Additional Revenue	PV Factor	PV of Revenue
1	$8,000	.877	$ 7,016
2	7,000	.769	5,383
3	6,000	.675	4,050
4	5,000	.592	2,960
5	4,000	.519	2,076
6	3,000	.456	1,368
7	2,000	.400	800
PV of Revenue Stream			$23,653

d. The present value would be lower because the larger payments occur later, when the present value factors are smaller.

Direct Your Learning

Applying Cash Flow Analysis

Educational Objectives

After learning the content of this assignment, you should be able to:

1. Explain how the recognition of expected losses alters the cash flows of a capital investment proposal.

2. Describe the effect that various risk control techniques have on net cash flows.

3. Calculate the net present value and the internal rate of return on a capital investment proposal that uses various risk control techniques.

4. Describe the effect that various risk financing techniques have on net cash flows.

5. Calculate the net present value and the internal rate of return on a capital investment proposal that uses various risk financing techniques.

6. Describe the effect that a combination of risk management techniques has on net cash flows.

7. Calculate the net present value and the internal rate of return on a capital investment proposal that uses a combination of risk management techniques.

8. Explain how to consider uncertainty in cash flow analysis.

9. Select the risk management technique that offers the highest net present value and internal rate of return for a given capital investment proposal.

10. Define or describe each of the Key Words and Phrases for this assignment.

Study Materials

Required Reading:
▶ Risk Assessment
  • Chapter 14

Study Aids:
▶ SMART Online Practice Exams
▶ SMART Study Aids
  • Review Notes and Flash Cards— Assignment 14

Outline

▶ **Recognizing Cash Flows Related to Risk Management Techniques**
   A. Cash Flows When Expected Losses Are Ignored
   B. Cash Flows Recognizing Expected Losses

▶ **Recognizing Cash Flows Related to Risk Control Techniques**
   A. Avoidance
   B. Prevention or Reduction of Losses
   C. Separation of Loss Exposures

▶ **Recognizing Cash Flows Related to Risk Financing Techniques**
   A. Loss Transfer Through a Captive Insurer
   B. Loss Transfer Through an Unrelated Insurer
   C. Loss Transfer Through a Hold-Harmless Agreement
   D. Loss Transfer Through Hedging (Business Risks)
   E. Loss Retention With Current Funding (Current Expenses)
   F. Loss Retention With Current Funding
      (An Unfunded Reserve)
   G. Loss Retention With Pre-Funding (A Funded Reserve)
   H. Loss Retention With Post-Funding (Borrowed Funds)

▶ **Recognizing Cash Flows Related to Combined Risk Management Techniques**

▶ **Considering Uncertainty in Cash Flow Analysis**

▶ **Using Cash Flow Analysis to Select Risk Management Techniques**

▶ **Summary**

 If you find your attention drifting, take a short break to regain your focus.

For each assignment, you should define or describe each of the Key Words and Phrases and answer each of the Review and Application Questions.

Educational Objective 1

Explain how the recognition of expected losses alters the cash flows of a capital investment proposal.

Review Questions

1-1.   When a risk management professional is considering the financial effects of an investment or activity on an organization, what should his or her cash flow analysis incorporate? (p. 14.5)

1-2.   Why is it important for management to recognize potential accidental losses when considering the financial effects of an investment or activity? (p. 14.7)

1-3.   What does the recognition of accidental losses in cash flow analysis enable a risk management professional to do with regard to risk management techniques? (p. 14.9)

Educational Objective 2

Describe the effect that various risk control techniques have on net cash flows.

Review Questions

2-1.   Under what circumstance might an organization choose avoidance as a risk control technique? (pp. 14.9–14.10)

2-2.   Does prevention or reduction of losses always increase the NPV and IRR on a particular capital investment proposal? (p. 14.11)

2-3.   What effect does separation of loss exposures have on the frequency and the severity of possible losses? (p. 14.11)

Educational Objective 3

Calculate the net present value and the internal rate of return on a capital investment proposal that uses various risk control techniques.

Review Questions

3-1.   What effect does the initial cost of a risk control technique have on the initial investment of a proposal? (pp. 14.11–14.12)

3-2.   What effect does the initial cost of a risk control technique have on the depreciation of a proposal? (p. 14.12)

3-3.   How are the continuing costs of a risk control technique accounted for in cash flow analysis? (p. 14.12)

Educational Objective 4

Describe the effect that various risk financing techniques have on net cash flows.

Key Word or Phrase

Loss adjustment expenses (p. 14.22)

Review Questions

4-1. Compared with retention, does using the risk financing technique of insurance increase or decrease the NPV and IRR of a proposal? (p. 14.14)

4-2. Explain how an organization can stabilize (reduce variation in, not necessarily increase or decrease) its annual net cash flows through hedging. (p. 14.18)

4-3. Explain whether the cash outflows associated with retaining losses as current expenses are identical to those associated with retaining losses through an unfunded reserve. (p. 14.23)

Educational Objective 5

Calculate the net present value and the internal rate of return on a capital investment proposal that uses various risk financing techniques.

Review Questions

5-1. What effect do the administrative expenses of a risk financing technique have on the NCF of a proposal? (p. 14.24)

5-2. What effect does the interest payment on retention with borrowed funds have on the NCF of a proposal? (p. 14.26)

5-3. What effect does retention with borrowed funds have on differential cash revenues of a proposal? (p. 14.28)

Educational Objective 6

Describe the effect that a combination of risk management techniques has on net cash flows.

Review Questions

6-1. Describe the financial benefits of accurate loss projections to an organization using a funded reserve. (p. 14.27)

6-2. Identify the effects on the initial investment, cash inflows, and cash outflows when an organization retains losses through a funded reserve. (p. 14.27)

6-3. What effect does the use of separation have on an organization's financial resources? (p. 14.31)

Educational Objective 7

Calculate the net present value and the internal rate of return on a capital investment proposal that uses a combination of risk management techniques.

Review Questions

7-1. What effect does a funded reserve have on the initial investment of a proposal? (p. 14.28)

7-2. What effect does a funded reserve have on the differential cash revenues of a proposal? (p. 14.28)

7-3. What effect does separation have on the funded reserve of a proposal? (p. 14.29)

Educational Objective 8

Explain how to consider uncertainty in cash flow analysis.

Review Questions

8-1.   What effects of retaining risk might an organization need to identify and quantify when deciding whether to retain large loss exposures? (pp. 14.31–14.32)

8-2.   Describe the "cost of uncertainty." (p. 14.32)

8-3.   Describe the steps in quantifying the uncertain costs of large losses when an organization performs a cash flow analysis of risk management technique alternatives. (p. 14.32)

Educational Objective 9

Select the risk management technique that offers the highest net present value and internal rate of return for a given capital investment proposal.

Review Questions

9-1. Describe the NPV and IRR decision criteria used by risk management professionals in cash flow analysis. (p. 14.34)

9-2. Identify an organizational goal that is taken into account by the NPV and IRR decision criteria regarding risk management decisions? (p. 14.34)

9-3. Do the NPV and IRR decision criteria take into account any other organizational goals regarding risk management decisions? (pp. 14.34–14.36)

Application Questions

9-4. A construction firm has just purchased for $18,000 a truck that is expected to generate a before-tax annual net cash flow of $10,000 in each of the six years of its useful life, after which the truck is expected to have no salvage value. This expected annual net cash flow does not include any allowance for possible damage to the truck.

Because the truck is to be used on and off public roads, it is particularly subject to physical damage from both traffic and construction accidents. The annual amount of physical damage to this truck is described by the following probability distribution:

Probability	Annual Damage to Truck
.60	$ 0
.30	1,000
.06	5,000
.04	18,000

a. What is the annual expected value of the physical damage to this truck? Show your calculations.

b. Assume, regardless of your answer in (a), that the annual expected value of physical damage to this truck is $1,400 and that the firm plans to retain any physical damage losses to the truck by paying them as current expenses. Refer to the following excerpt from a table entitled "Present Value of $1 Received Annually at the End of Each of n Periods" to determine whether the use of this truck and the retaining of the annual expected value of physical damage to the truck will generate an after-tax internal rate of return greater than the 22 percent rate of return the firm averages on its other assets. Assume straight-line depreciation and a 50 percent income tax rate. Show your calculations.

n	18%	20%	22%	24%
6	3.50	3.33	3.17	3.02

9-5. Milker Corporation is considering buying Prairie View Farm, a 160-acre family-operated dairy farm located near a busy state highway in a suburban area. Over 90 percent of the farm's $300,000 annual revenue is derived from sales of unprocessed milk and homemade ice cream. Two hundredths of one percent (0.0002) of the 180,000 retail customers who each year buy milk at Prairie View Farm claim to have been poisoned by the milk. Although the farm's management believes that any poisoning is primarily caused by impurities already in the containers that customers bring to be filled, the fact that Prairie View milk is unprocessed leaves the farm particularly vulnerable to liability. Therefore, rather than go to court, the farm has been paying an average of $300 as a settlement to each person who claims to have been poisoned by the milk.

a. Calculate, or show how to calculate, the annual expected value of the settlement payments that the farm has been making to customers claiming to have been poisoned.

b. Milker Corporation is considering buying Prairie View Farm for $1,000,000. Milker believes that the farm will be productive for fifteen years and then will shut down and have no salvage value. Milker's management wants an internal rate of return of at least 18 percent. Determine if Milker should buy this farm. (Take into account the cost of expected losses, and assume Milker's tax rate is 35 percent.)

c. Assume all the same facts as in part (b) with the additional concern that Milker's management believes that the uncertainty regarding liability needs to be factored into the analysis. Milker's risk management professional has determined that the cost of uncertainty regarding liability should be $20,000 per year. Should Milker purchase the farm?

d. For an additional $100,000, Milker can purchase equipment with the farm that will process its milk (no poisonings) for the next 15 years, after which the equipment will have no salvage value. Calculate the internal rate of return.

e. Calculate the internal rate of return if, instead of purchasing the processing equipment, Milker purchased an annual general liability policy that would cost $35,000 per year in premium and cover all liability claims.

f. Rank Milker's choices from highest to lowest based on IRR for each of the following choices: buy Prairie View, buy Prairie View and equipment, buy Prairie View and insurance, do nothing.

Answers to Assignment 14 Questions

NOTE: These answers are provided to give students a basic understanding of acceptable types of responses. They often are not the only valid answers and are not intended to provide an exhaustive response to the questions.

Educational Objective 1

1-1. To adequately consider the financial effects on an investment or activity on an organization, cash flow analysis should incorporate the estimated differential after-tax net cash flows related to all the proposal's costs and benefits, including any risk management techniques. The cash flow analysis should explicitly recognize the one-time costs of implementing risk management techniques as well as any continuing risk management costs.

1-2. It is important to recognize potential accidental losses because they affect the net cash flows. Changes to the net cash flows can alter the NPV and IRR of an investment proposal and, ultimately, the decision as to which proposal an organization will devote its resources.

1-3. The recognition of accidental losses in a proposal's cash flow analysis enables a risk management professional to analyze the effects of various risk control and risk financing techniques on those accidental losses.

Educational Objective 2

2-1. An organization might choose avoidance if the NPV or IRR from an activity using the appropriate risk management techniques (other than avoidance) falls below the minimum amount necessary to justify acceptance of the proposal.

2-2. No, loss prevention or reduction techniques do not necessarily increase the NPV or IRR. In practice, it depends on the details of the particular proposal.

2-3. Separation increases the number of loss exposure units, which often increases the frequency of losses that may occur but reduces the severity of those losses.

Educational Objective 3

3-1. The initial cost of a risk control technique is added to the initial investment of a proposal, increasing the amount of the initial investment.

3-2. Since the initial cost of a risk control technique is added to the initial investment and is a capital expenditure, it can be depreciated over the life of the proposal. Therefore, the initial cost of the risk control technique increases the differential depreciation.

3-3. The continuing costs of a risk control technique appear as a differential cash expense and are subtracted from differential cash revenues.

Educational Objective 4

4-1. Using the risk financing technique of insurance usually produces a lower NPV or IRR than retention. The amount of reduction depends on the size of the insurer's premium loading for its expenses and profit and any additional costs of retention.

4-2. Organizations that use hedging sacrifice some or all of the potential net revenue gain in exchange for protection against price changes that can cause a loss.

4-3. Except for some possible extra administrative costs, the cash outflows associated with retaining losses as current expense and cash outflows associated with retaining losses through an unfunded reserve are identical. An unfunded reserve is merely an accounting recognition of anticipated expense.

Educational Objective 5

5-1. Administrative expenses are included in differential cash expenses and are subtracted from the differential cash revenues. Therefore, administrative expenses increase differential cash expenses.

5-2. The interest payment is added to the loan amount and is included in the differential cash expenses that are subtracted from the differential cash revenues. Therefore, interest payments increase differential cash expenses.

5-3. Borrowing to pay for the expected losses releases internal capital to use in operations, which will generate a rate of return equal to the organization's cost of capital.

Educational Objective 6

6-1. The financial benefits of accurate loss projections to an organization using a funded reserve include the following:
- Reduced amount of funded reserve needed to retain losses
- Funds freed up to be used for other investment opportunities

6-2. Retaining losses through a funded reserve has the following NCF effects:
- Increases the initial investment in an asset or activity
- Does not change the cash outflows arising from loss payments
- Gives the potential for cash inflows in the form of earnings on the fund held in the reserve

6-3. Using separation reduces the amount of financial resources an organization might need to commit to ensure losses can be paid from available funds.

Educational Objective 7

7-1. The amount of the funded reserve is added to the initial investment but is not depreciated over the life of the proposal. Therefore, it increases the initial investment but has no effect on depreciation.

7-2. The amount earned on the funded reserve is added to the differential cash inflows. Because it is a speculative investment, the amount could be positive or negative. Therefore, it could increase or decrease cash inflows.

7-3. Separation reduces the necessary funded reserve because separation reduces the severity of losses that may occur.

Educational Objective 8

8-1.   An organization might need to identify and quantify the following effects of retaining large loss exposures:

- Increased risk to managers, employees, customers, and suppliers

- Expected value of legal and related costs if large losses prevent fulfillment of contractual obligations

- Possible increases in the cost of raising funds and possible loss of valuable investment opportunities

- Possible increases in expected income taxes because retention plans are not generally tax deductible

8-2.   The "cost of uncertainty" is a subjectively assigned price of an expected cost that is difficult to measure. It is used in cash flow analysis of a risk management technique.

8-3.   The steps in quantifying the uncertain costs of large losses when an organization performs a cash flow analysis of risk management technique alternatives are as follows:

- Assign a subjective estimate of the cost of uncertainty to each alternative risk management technique

- Deduct the assigned cost of uncertainty from the after-tax net cash inflow (or add it to the after-tax net cash outflow) for each period it is used

- Calculate the NPV and IRR for each technique using the adjusted net cash flows

Educational Objective 9

9-1.   Risk management professionals use the following criteria when using cash flow analysis to evaluate possible expected accidental losses in the selection of risk management techniques:

- NPV criteria—an organization should prefer the risk management technique that promises the highest positive NPV for the proposal to which that technique is applied.

- IRR criteria—an organization should select the risk management technique that promises the highest IRR above the minimum rate of return on the proposal to which that technique is applied.

9-2.   The NPV and IRR decision criteria enable an organization to maximize its value through risk management decisions that support the pre-loss goal of economy.

9-3.   No, the NPV and IRR decision criteria are purely financial calculations and have no bearing on decision making regarding other organizational goals.

9-4.   a.

Probability	Damage	Expected Value
.60	$ 0	$ 0
.30	1,000	300
.06	5,000	300
.04	18,000	720
Expected value		$1,320

b.   NCF Calculations

Differential Cash Revenues		$10,000
Less: Differential Expenses (except income taxes)		
Expected losses		($ 1,400)
Before-Tax NCF:		$ 8,600
Less: Differential Income taxes:		
Before-Tax NCF:	$8,600	
Less: Differential Depreciation		
expense ($18,000 ÷ 6 years)	($3,000)	
Taxable Income	$5,600	
Income Taxes (50%)		($2,800)
After-Tax NCF:		$5,800

Present value factor = $18,000 ÷ $5,800 = 3.103.

Therefore the IRR over 6 years is between 22 percent and 24 percent, or more than 22 percent.

9-5. a.   180,000 customers × 0.0002 = 36 customers.

        Annual expected value = 36 × $300

                                = $10,800.

b.   As the cash flow analysis produces a positive NPV and an IRR in excess of the required rate of return, Milker should purchase the farm.

NCF Calculations

Differential Cash Revenues		$300,000
Less: Differential Cash Expenses		
(liability settlements; except income taxes)		($ 10,800)
Before-Tax NCF:		$289,200
Less: Differential Income taxes:		
Before-Tax NCF:	$289,200	
Less: Differential Depreciation		
expense ($1,000,000 ÷ 15 years)	($ 66,667)	
Taxable Income	$222,533	
Income Taxes (35%)		($ 77,887)
After-Tax NCF:		$211,313

NCF Analysis

Factors:

Initial Investment	$1,000,000
Life of Project	15 years
Differential Annual after-tax NCF	$ 211,313
Minimum acceptable rate of return (annual)	18.00%

Analysis by NPV:

PV of differential NCF ($211,313 × 5.1)	$1,077,698
Less: PV of initial investment	($1,000,000)
NPV:	$ 77,698

Analysis by IRR:

PVF = Initial Investment ÷ Differential NCF

PVF = $1,000,000 ÷ $211,313 = 4.732.

Interpolation to find the IRR (*r*):

	Rate of Return	PVF	PVF
	18.00%	5.092	
	r		4.732
	20.00%	4.675	
Differences:	2.00%	0.417	0.360

r = 18% + [(0.360 ÷ 0.417) × 2%]

   = 18% + 1.73%

   = 19.73%.

c. As the cash flow analysis produces a negative NPV and an IRR below the required rate of return, Milker should not purchase the farm.

NCF Calculations

Differential Cash Revenues		$300,000
Less: Differential Cash Expenses		
(liability settlements; except income taxes)		($ 10,800)
Before-Tax NCF:		$289,200
Less: Differential Income taxes:		
Before-Tax NCF:	$289,200	
Less: Differential Depreciation		
expense ($1,000,000 ÷ 15 years)	($ 66,667)	
Taxable Income	$222,533	
Income Taxes (35%)		($ 77,887)
After-Tax NCF:		$211,313
Less: Cost of Uncertainty:		($ 20,000)
		$191,313

NCF Analysis

Factors:

Initial Investment	$1,000,000
Life of Project	15 years
Differential Annual after-tax NCF	$ 191,313
Minimum acceptable rate of return (annual)	18.00%

Analysis by NPV:

PV of differential NCF ($191,313 × 5.1)	$ 975,698
Less: PV of initial investment	($1,000,000)
NPV:	($ 24,302)

Analysis by IRR:

PVF = Initial Investment ÷ Differential NCF

PVF = $1,000,000 ÷ $191,313 = 5.227.

Interpolation to find the IRR (*r*):

Rate of Return	PVF	PVF
16.00%	5.575	
r		5.227
18.00%	5.092	
Differences: 2.00%	0.483	0.348

$r = 16\% + [(0.348 \div 0.483) \times 2\%]$

$= 16\% + 1.44\%$

$= 17.44\%$.

d.   NCF Calculations

Differential Cash Revenues		$300,000
Less: Differential Cash Expenses (liability settlements; except income taxes)		$ 0
Before-Tax NCF:		$300,000
Less: Differential Income taxes:		
Before-Tax NCF:	$300,000	
Less: Differential Depreciation expense ($1,100,000 ÷ 15 years)	($ 73,333)	
Taxable Income	$226,667	
Income Taxes (35%)		($ 79,333)
After-Tax NCF:		$220,667

<u>NCF Analysis</u>

Factors:

Initial Investment	$1,100,000
Life of Project	15 years
Differential Annual after-tax NCF	$ 220,667
Minimum acceptable rate of return (annual)	18.00%

Analysis by IRR:

PVF = Initial Investment ÷ Differential NCF

PVF = $1,100,000 ÷ $220,667 = 4.985.

Interpolation to find the IRR (*r*):

	Rate of Return	PVF	PVF
	18.00%	5.092	
	r		4.985
	20.00%	4.675	
Differences:	2.00%	0.417	0.107

$r = 18\% + [(0.107 ÷ 0.417) × 2\%]$

$\quad = 18\% + 0.51\%$

$\quad = 18.51\%.$

e. <u>NCF Calculations</u>

Differential Cash Revenues		$300,000
Less: Differential Cash Expenses		
(liability settlements; except income taxes)		($ 35,000)
Before-Tax NCF:		$265,000
Less: Differential Income taxes:		
Before-Tax NCF:	$265,000	
Less: Differential Depreciation		
expense ($1,000,000 ÷ 15 years)	($ 66,667)	
Taxable Income	$198,333	
Income Taxes (35%)		($ 69,417)
After-Tax NCF:		$195,583

<u>NCF Analysis</u>

Factors:

Initial Investment	$1,000,000
Life of Project	15 years
Differential Annual after-tax NCF	$ 195,583
Minimum acceptable rate of return (annual)	18.00%

Analysis by NPV:

PV of differential NCF ($195,583 × 5.1)	$ 997,473
Less: PV of initial investment	($1,000,000)
NPV:	($ 2,527)

Analysis by IRR:

PVF = Initial Investment ÷ Differential NCF

PVF = $1,000,000 ÷ $195,585 = 5.113.

Interpolation to find the IRR (*r*):

Rate of Return	PVF	PVF
16.00%	5.575	
r		5.113
18.00%	5.092	
Differences: 2.00%	0.483	0.462

$r = 16\% + [(0.462 ÷ 0.483) × 2\%]$

$\quad = 16\% + 1.91\%$

$\quad = 17.91\%.$

f.

Choice	IRR
Buy farm and equipment	18.51%
Do nothing	18.00%
Buy farm and insurance	17.91%
Buy farm	17.44%

▶▶

Exam Information

About Institute Exams

Exam questions are based on the Educational Objectives stated in the course guide and textbook. The exam is designed to measure whether you have met those Educational Objectives. The exam does not test every Educational Objective. Instead, it tests over a balanced sample of Educational Objectives.

How to Prepare for Institute Exams

What can you do to prepare for an Institute exam? Students who pass Institute exams do the following:

▶ Use the assigned study materials. Focus your study on the Educational Objectives presented at the beginning of each course guide assignment. Thoroughly read the textbook and any other assigned materials, and then complete the course guide exercises. Choose a study method that best suits your needs; for example, participate in a traditional class, online class, or informal study group; or study on your own. Use the Institutes' SMART Study Aids (if available) for practice and review. If this course has an associated SMART Online Practice Exams product, you will find an access code on the inside back cover of this course guide. This access code allows you to print (in PDF format) a full practice exam and to take additional online practice exams that will simulate an actual credentialing exam.

▶ Become familiar with the types of test questions asked on the exam. The practice exam in this course guide or in the SMART Online Practice Exams product will help you understand the different types of questions you will encounter on the exam.

▶ Maximize your test-taking time. Successful students use the sample exam in the course guide or in the SMART Online Practice Exams product to practice pacing themselves. Learning how to manage your time during the exam ensures that you will complete all of the test questions in the time allotted.

Types of Exam Questions

The exam for this course consists of objective questions of several types.

The Correct-Answer Type

In this type of question, the question stem is followed by four responses, one of which is absolutely correct. Select the *correct* answer.

> Which one of the following persons evaluates requests for insurance to determine which applicants are accepted and which are rejected?
>
> a.   The premium auditor
>
> b.   The loss control representative
>
> c.   The underwriter
>
> d.   The risk manager

The Best-Answer Type

In this type of question, the question stem is followed by four responses, only one of which is best, given the statement made or facts provided in the stem. Select the *best* answer.

> Several people within an insurer might be involved in determining whether an applicant for insurance is accepted. Which one of the following positions is primarily responsible for determining whether an applicant for insurance is accepted?
>
> a.   The loss control representative
>
> b.   The customer service representative
>
> c.   The underwriter
>
> d.   The premium auditor

The Incomplete-Statement or Sentence-Completion Type

In this type of question, the last part of the question stem consists of a portion of a statement rather than a direct question. Select the phrase that *correctly* or *best* completes the sentence.

Residual market plans designed for individuals who are unable to obtain insurance on their personal property in the voluntary market are called

a. VIN plans.

b. Self-insured retention plans.

c. Premium discount plans.

d. FAIR plans.

"All of the Above" Type

In this type of question, only one of the first three answers could be correct, or all three might be correct, in which case the best answer would be "All of the above." Read all the answers and select the *best* answer.

When a large commercial insured's policy is up for renewal, who is likely to provide input to the renewal decision process?

a. The underwriter

b. The loss control representative

c. The producer

d. All of the above

"All of the following, EXCEPT:" Type

In this type of question, responses include three correct answers and one answer that is incorrect or is clearly the least correct. Select the *incorrect* or *least correct* answer.

All of the following adjust insurance claims, EXCEPT:

a. Insurer claim representatives

b. Premium auditors

c. Producers

d. Independent adjusters